COLONIAL
VIRGINIA'S
War Against Piracy

COLONIAL VIRGINIA'S
VIRGINIA'S
War Against Piracy

The Governor
&
the Buccaneer

JEREMY R. MOSS

THE
History
PRESS

Published by The History Press
Charleston, SC
www.historypress.com

First published 2022

Manufactured in the United States

ISBN 9781467152198

Library of Congress Control Number: 2022933380

For my wife, Katy, and children.
You are the world's greatest treasure.

CONTENTS

CONTENTS

PREFACE

My love for history of the Golden Age of Piracy is a relatively new phenomenon. Before researching and writing my first book, *The Life and Tryals of the Gentleman Pirate, Major Stede Bonnet*, my exposure to pirates, buccaneers and privateers was limited.

As a kid, I loved playing *Pirates!* on the original Nintendo gaming system, and for a short while in my teenage years, I considered attending the University of the West Indies in Kingston, Jamaica (more because of my early love for Bob Marley than any interest in pirates). I had, of course, read *Treasure Island*, seen *The Goonies*, *Hook*, *The Princess Bride* and *Cutthroat Island*, but although I hate to admit it, I have still not seen all of the *Pirates of the Caribbean* movies.

Then, five years ago, I got hooked. While visiting a small coffee ship in Virginia Beach, Virginia (Three Ships, try the biscuits), I picked up a small book of local ghost stories. While flipping through its pages, I was particularly enchanted by stories of Blackbeard the pirate, who, like other pirates, as I would learn, shared a rich history with Virginia and Virginia Beach (some of which is discussed in this book). I was immediately "all in" and searched for more stories of Blackbeard and his compatriots.

On one hand, I was surprised by the small number of scholarly, historical works about pirates. I expected hundreds would have been written over the three hundred years since piracy's golden age. Instead, I found only dozens. Nonetheless, I consumed every book and article I could find.

As I read, I continued to come across references to lesser-known compatriots of the pirate greats and was exposed to dozens of stories in which larger-than-life characters jumped out of the historical record and proved that sometimes, real life can be stranger than fiction.

Even with a sparse historical record for many pirates, collections of original source documents are beginning to make their way onto the internet in scanned and translated form. One of the most significant resources in telling this story about the arrogant and brash Governor Francis Nicholson and the (somewhat) more caring and suave buccaneer Louis Guittar is the hundred-plus-page handwritten trial transcript that still survives, preserved in the British archives, of three pirates who sailed with Guittar. Through the power of the internet—despite the global pandemic—I was able to get my hands on the digital document.

This handwritten transcript is a unique resource, providing contemporaneous, firsthand accounts from several members of Guittar's crew, including Guittar himself. The transcript provided me a crash-course in paleography (the study of historic writing), and my transcription, done on nights and weekends after my three young sons went to bed, took weeks to complete. Combined with letters from governors, ship captains and other colonial and English officials, along with secondhand sources, I was able to piece together what I think is a fascinating story of the governor and buccaneer.

In writing this book, my philosophy has been to seek the original source whenever possible. This book contains a number of quotes from these original sources. These sources may have been originally identified in any of the modern works that have influenced my viewpoint on Governor Nicholson, Captain Guittar and pirates generally.

Punctuation, spelling and, in some cases, diction, may have been revised from their original sources to increase readability and comprehension. At times, however, original punctuation, spelling and diction have been left in its original form. Dates, whenever listed, match their original source.

With that, we begin the story of the beginning of colonial Virginia's war on piracy.

ACKNOWLEDGEMENTS

In many ways, I am still getting my "sea legs" under me. With this, my second book, I have become much more settled into my life as emerging author and freelance historian. This book and others I've written are labors of love, and at times, I admit that my love for research and writing ebbs and flows.

But what has not ebbed is the love and support I have received along the way.

First, I must acknowledge you, the reader of my book. Ultimately, I write for you. As I find the stories in history that must be told, I have you in mind. I hope that you are entertained and informed by my work and want to thank you for buying, borrowing or, in a truly piratical way, stealing this book and reading it.

I would be remiss to not also thank my family, especially my wife, Katy, and friends, who have all heard way too many stories about pirates over the last half decade. It is not lost on me that my family and friends have supported me by buying my books, liking my posts on social media and passing my books along to others who may enjoy them.

I'd also like to extend my gratitude to my extended "crew," whom I've met along the way. I've had tremendous love and support from so many within the historical communities that I'm reticent to share specifics in case I may inadvertently forget someone. A special thanks to the teams at the Mariners' Museum and Park, the Hampton History Museum, Old Baldy Lighthouse and Smith Island Museum and the Federal Point Historic Preservation

Society. Thank you also to the dozens of book clubs, Rotary clubs and historical societies that have welcomed me to their meetings.

And thank you to the others within the community of academics, scholars and writers who are constantly advancing scholarship about piracy. In no particular order, I am constantly inspired, engaged, challenged and informed by people (many of whom I now consider friends), like Dr. Jaime Goodall, Dr. Manushag "Nush" Powell, Dr. Rebecca Simon, Eric Jay Dolin, Colin Woodard, Dr. Mark G. Hanna, Matt McLaine, Joshua Provan and Laura Duncombe.

1

"I KNOW HOW TO GOVERN"

Colonel Francis Nicholson returned to Jamestown, Virginia, in December 1698 to an isolating and solemn reception. Having spent almost six years as the governor of the Maryland colony, Nicholson should have been ecstatic about the opportunity to return to Virginia. Nicholson abruptly left his previous appointment as Virginia's lieutenant governor in 1692, when his former friend and mentor Sir Edmund Andros was appointed governor of the colony.

Nicholson's abrupt departure from his post was not unusual behavior for the former lieutenant governor, even though Nicholson knew Andros well (Nicholson had known Andros for at least six years prior to 1692 and had served on the Dominion of New England's Council under Andros previously). No, instead it was simply another instance of the "flaring temper" of a man who was "subject to fits of passion in which he lost all reason."[1]

Nonetheless, Andros's poor health and political pressures (stemming mainly from a dispute with Dr. James Blair) reopened the door for Nicholson's return to Virginia.[2]

Nicholson arrived in the beginning of a typical Jamestown, Virginia winter—so cold that, as the early, influential settler John Smith said, a "dogge would scarce have indured it." Making an already brutal winter worse, in 1698, the world was still locked in the Little Ice Age, enduring consistent periods of exceptionally severe winters, with extreme cold weather and frost.

Not all was well when Nicholson entered the statehouse in Jamestown on December 9, 1698, to communicate his commission as governor and to

John Smith and Norris Peters Co., Virginia. *Courtesy of the Library of Congress, Geography and Map Division.*

take the oaths of office. Portions of the Jamestown State House, Virginia's fourth in Jamestown in seventy years, had been burned in a fire only a few weeks before Nicholson's arrival. Rumors of arson swirled around the burned remains.

Only half of the Virginia Council were present when Colonel Nicholson communicated his commission as the new governor (then publishing the commission in the statehouse as public notice), unceremoniously taking the oath of office and swearing in Benjamin Harrison and Matthew Page as new members of the council.[3]

Throughout the council meeting, Nicholson had difficulty concentrating, thinking instead of the visit earlier in the day from his old friend Dr. James Blair. Blair and Nicholson would have a complicated history of governance that ebbed and flowed between friendship and animosity and success and failure.

Excited for Nicholson's return to Virginia, Dr. Blair delivered Nicholson's commission to him along with several letters from bishops and "other friends in England." Each of the letters, as Nicholson would see, recommended "moderation" in his governance of Virginia. Francis Nicholson had developed a complicated reputation.

Nicholson was a professional government executive, having served previously on the Council of the Dominion of New England and as the governor of the Dominion of New England, lieutenant governor of New York, lieutenant governor of Virginia, as a member of the executive council and lieutenant governor of Maryland and as governor of Maryland.[4]

Francis Nicholson was the "model governor general who dominated many royal colonies."[5] Nicholson was routinely praised and "proudly remembered" (especially among Marylanders), as a city-builder, a devout Anglican, a promoter of the church and education, a resolute soldier and a zealous suppressor of piracy and illegal trade.[6]

While governor of Maryland, Nicholson developed the plan for the city of Annapolis (which would become Maryland's capital city), and the statehouse and brick-constructed free school were constructed during his term.[7] At the end of his term, a joint letter was given to Nicholson with signatures from members of the colonial council, the justices of the provincial court, thirty-four members of the Maryland House of Delegates, the grand jury and chancellor, heaping praise on the outgoing governor.

Nicholson's "time, money and energy, were given to the church not less than to the government."[8]

The letter read:

> *That your conduct over us in this place, your great care and study has been to promote the practice of piety and worship of Almighty God by erecting churches, schools and nurseries of learning, both for reforming manners and education of youth, wherein you have been, not only a large contributor, but an intelligent promoter, together with your integrity of maintaining His Majesty's honor and authority in this province, your care in providing arms and military discipline of it; your regulating and happy settlement of the civil constitution, both as to the courts of justice, and in bringing us out of debt, which the public was in, into a condition clear of debt and money in bank; by your promotion of good laws to such purposes, your great care to cause speedy justice to be administered to all persons, your pious and jst [sic], your noble and benevolent carriage in all things deserve better pens than ours and would take up more paper than this to recount. Be pleased therefore, honorable Sir, to accept our humble acknowledgements for the same, as the just through slender tribute of an obliged people to a*

generous, good governor, praying God to bless you in all *your pious and noble undertakings with happiness and success, so pray your humble and obliged servants.*[9]

Praise continued for Nicholson,

The governor is very well beloved by the whole country, but because his time is over, they think of another governor and do desire earnestly to have His Excellency Nicholson, who indeed is a most eminent governor; and as fit (as said to me, once, Your Lordship), to be a bishop as to be a governor. If His Excellency was governor here, and Your Lordship would send here a good bishop with a severe observation of the canons of the church and eager for the salvation of souls, there would be a great alteration in the Church. Religion and piety should flourish presently, and we should be mighty glad and contented. When I do think with myself of Governor Nicholson, I do call him the right hand of God, the father of the church, and more, a father of the poor. An eminent bishop of that same character being sent over here with him, will make Hell tremble and settle the Church of England in these parts forever.[10]

Still yet, Governor Nicholson also had many enemies related mostly to his "impulsive and hasty temper, under the influence of which he was at times arbitrary and overbearing."[11] Complaints against Nicholson were varied, and he was claimed to:

- provoke the Natives to war and stir the English to insurrection to gain a reputation for loyalty;
- grieve and perplex his officers and others by illegal and arbitrary commands about frivolous affairs;
- alter and attempt to alter the constitution of government;
- press men's horses and boats in time of peace for his private and public use;
- issue proclamations, enjoining new oaths and penalties without authority of law;
- intimidate the people for seeking relief from his apparent oppression;
- require absolute obedience from the civil officers to his own particular orders without any reserve under great penalties; and
- require excessive bail in inconsiderable matters.[12]

James Blair, circa 1725. *From Wikimedia Commons.*

This sentiment seems to have defined Nicholson. He was revered by some as a devout protector (of the colonies and the church), despite his personality, and by others, he was seen as an overbearing, narcissistic egomaniac lacking any semblance of empathy.

Dr. Blair advocated for a more even approach to governance and iterated his support of the advice for moderation, which he described as "the best advice could be given at that time to a gentleman in his circumstances."[13]

As he read the letters, Nicholson's mood swung quickly from delight in seeing his old friend to anger. He thrust the letters toward Dr. Blair.

"What the devil do they mean to recommend moderation to me?" Nicholson questioned.

Blair answered calmly, "They are all of the opinion that this is the best advice that can be given to you, for Sir, they have seen the articles that were exhibited against Your Excellency by Captain Sly and judge all these ill things you are accused of as having proceeded from your passion, and they know that in Virginia, as you have many friends, so you also have diverse enemies of Sir Edmund Andros's party, and therefore, they are afraid of your resentments. I can't but be of their opinion that it is your best way to forgive and forget and to begin upon a new foot and to make yourself easy for everybody else."[14]

Nicholson "replied very hotly, 'I know how to govern Virginia and Maryland better than all the bishops in England. If I had not hampered them in Maryland and kept them under, I should never have been able to have Govern'd them."[15]

"Sir," Blair replied, "I don't pretend to understand Maryland, but if I know anything of Virginia, they are a good-natured, tractable people as any is in the world, and you may do anything with them by the way of civility, but you will never be able to manage them in that way you speak of by hampering and keeping them under."[16]

"You don't know any better; let me alone with them. I warrant you, I will manage them."[17]

Leaving it at that, Dr. Blair left Nicholson alone to calm down but tried to re-engage Nicholson six weeks later. Nicholson was even further resolved in thinking and "very stiff in his opinion."[18]

Blair again "urged to him the danger of losing assemblys and that if once he lost his interest there that he could not carry business for the king, the king would quickly come to think he was not a man for his turn."[19]

Nicholson was unpersuaded, curtly responding, "I know how to govern the country without assemblies."[20]

Nicholson's response startled Blair, but Blair was unable to bring Nicholson "off of it," to see the potential value in engaging the council, creating alliances and working the assembly.[21]

Nicholson would have none of it.

"Never open your mouth to me again in any manner related to the government," Nicholson chided. "Let me alone and meddle in your own business."[22]

"Yes, Sir," Blair readily promised, for he could tell Nicholson "was strongly bent on violent and arbitrary methods in which…[Blair] was resolved not to be concerned."[23]

The truth is, Virginia had changed, and perhaps Nicholson recognized that, even if he would not admit it to Blair. The first stock of men of "Virginia gentlemen" had been educated in England and were well accomplished in the law and their knowledge of the world.[24] Their descendants, however, were less so.

Blair would report later that Nicholson "governs us as if we were a company of galley slaves by continual roaring and thundering, cursing and swearing, base, abusive, billingsgate language to that degree that it is utterly incredible to those who have not been the spectators of it."[25] Blair was concerned that "the public peace of the colony…[is] endangered by Colonel Nicholson's temper."[26]

Blair went on to describe Nicholson as "exceedingly angry that anyone should be set over his head in Virginia" and found Nicholson to be "very apprehensive himself of the difficulty of his circumstances between the love of the people and the jealousy of the government." Nonetheless and perhaps after the opportunity to further consider his words, Blair relented that Nicholson was not an "enemy to the government" and expressed remorse for prior, more specific attacks on Nicholson, who, in Blair's words, deserved "encouragement or reward to one who deserves it as well as any governor that ever was in America."[27] Blair's view of Nicholson, like the public at large's (even today), was complicated, ebbing and flowing from disdain to appreciation.

Despite Nicholson's impetuous statements and personal attacks on his political opponents, Nicholson continued to be elevated to positions of relative power. Nicholson's brash and boisterous demeanor, abruptness of action and his unwillingness to back down from a fight may have been attractive to the relatively uneducated (or at least less educated) citizens of then-modern Virginia, whose personalities (and manners) had been forged in the crucible of a budding settlement, even if not attractive in the cosmopolitan streets of urban London. Perhaps then Nicholson was a bellwether of the changing culture of the time.

2

"A REMARKABLY SEASONED MILITARY OFFICER AND COLONIAL ADMINISTRATOR"

Before arriving in Jamestown in the winter of 1698, the governor had already compiled an impressive résumé in the English colonies, Europe and Africa and was a "remarkably seasoned military officer and colonial administrator, with extensive experience throughout England's continental colonies."[28]

In his early adult life, Nicholson gained significant experience in the military, with stations at army posts in Holland, Tangier (in North Africa) and England in his first ten years of service. Nicholson's army years would be formative, especially his service in the English army unit known as the Tangier Regiment.

In 1680, at the age of twenty-five, Francis Nicholson was appointed lieutenant while serving in Tangier. The Tangier Regiment was "infamous for its excesses in putting down Monmouth's Rebellion…and not at all a training ground for leaders respectful of the rights of Englishmen."[29] Nicholson's abrupt governance style was already on display in Tangier, telling "his subjects 'that they were dogs, and their wives were bitches; that he knew how to govern the Moors and would beat them into better manners.'"[30]

Nicholson's station in the "small, isolated, besieged, quarrelsome Tangier garrison" would serve to expand Nicholson's future political network as he served with Lieutenant Colonel Thomas Dongan (Tangier's lieutenant governor and Nicholson's predecessor in New York), Lieutenant Colonel Robert Needham (who would later serve in Nicholson's council under the dominion government in New York), William Smith (the last mayor of Tangier and future president of the New York Council), Alexander Spotswood (the future lieutenant governor of Virginia who was responsible for the killing of Edward Teach, also known as the pirate Blackbeard), Roger Elliott (the half brother of Spotswood, the future British general and governor of Gibraltar) and Colonel Francis Russell (the future governor of Barbados).[31]

In 1686, at the age of thirty-two, Nicholson was commissioned as a captain of a company of infantrymen and received orders to the dominion of New England (an area that spans from as far north as present-day Maine and as far south as New Jersey). Through his service to New England, Nicholson earned the favor of New England governor Sir Edmund Andros and was appointed lieutenant governor of the Dominion of New England on April 20, 1688, and given responsibility for New York. Nicholson's commission put on Nicholson a "speciall trust and confidence" in his "loyalty courage and [almost ironically] circumspection."

Governor Andros's appointment was, at least in part, due to his support of the Duke of York when he backed King James II in 1685 (the year before Andros was appointed by James II as governor).

It was in this post as lieutenant governor of New England that Nicholson was first exposed to the pirates of the colonial era. In August 1688, only four months into Nicholson's post as lieutenant governor, Nicholson was sent (by land) along with Captain George of the HMS *Rose* (by sea) to recover a captured New England fishing boat in Rhode Island.

Nicholson would soon capture "eight men supposed to be pirates" and would describe the capture in an August 31, 1688 letter to Colonial Secretary William Blathwayt.[32] Through interrogation, Nicholson and Captain George learned that these pirates had sailed with a Captain Peterson, the master of a ten-gun barco longo with seventy men, that had been spotted in Rhode Island over the summer. Although Peterson was gone by the time Captain George and Nicholson arrived in Rhode Island, Nicholson was relentless in his search and continued inquiries about the pirates and their business in the colony.

Stated most simply, a "pirate" is a person who robs or steals at sea. *Pirate* is a generic team, however, and in 1688 could be used to describe any "traytors…thieves, robbers, murtherers and confederates upon the sea…or in or upon any other haven, river or creek."[33] These men (and women) operated outside of the law, but most did not lead "a life of continual isolation."[34]

To survive and perpetuate their trade, pirates relied on a network of relatively safe harbors and supportive traders and merchants. One of these merchants described the necessity of the pirate/merchant relationship:

> *The pirates themselves have often told me that if they had not been supported by the traders from* [mainland colonies] *with ammunition and provisions according to their directions, they could never have become so formidable.*[35]

And because much of what was taken by pirates were provisions, ammunition, sails and rigging and other merchandise, the pirates relied on merchants to monetize their plunder. It was money, for most pirates, that motivated their bad deeds.

Nicholson was aware of this motivation and need and began to inquire about illicit cash flows that led to a group of Rhode Island men—merchants—who traded with Peterson. With eight pirates already in captivity, many colonial administrators may have ignored the merchants—but not Nicholson.

Nicholson was dedicated to breaking down the illicit trade network, and at Nicholson's urging, Governor Andros ordered a court to try the merchants. Ultimately, the grand jury threw out the bill against the merchants, releasing them.

Still, Nicholson had confiscated two ketches (two-masted sailing vessels) for trading with Peterson and was holding the ships, their masters and several of their men in prison in Salem, Massachusetts.[36]

Nicholson had proven himself to be a relentless pirate hunter and law enforcer.

3

"PROFLIGATE MEN AND THEIR BARBAROUS ACTIONS"

As Nicholson settled into his service as governor of Virginia in 1698, his attention was soon directed to securing Virginia's shoreline borders and adjacent waters. Nicholson brought back to Virginia "his hatred of piracy and intolerance for the leaders and merchant communities of other English American colonies who openly winked at and occasionally outright supported pirates."[37]

The year prior, in 1697, the Nine Years' War had concluded with the signing of the Treaty of Ryswick. British trade with the colonies suffered tremendously from harassment by the French fleet during the war, with attacks by both French privateers (those mercenary sailors operating with permission of the French government, by letter of marque, to attack vessels at sea) and by pirates.[38]

These pirates were of mixed origin, with some of French origin and others coming directly from the British colonies. During the Nine Years' War (and, at times, after) men were press-ganged into the crews of British ships and subjected to brutal treatment from British officers. Many of these men deserted their ships upon reaching colonial ports, and those men were easily persuaded to join pirate crews that had a comparatively low risk and a tremendous upside. In fact, "toward the close of the war, which ended at the peace of Ryswick, British pirates fitted out from British Colonies practically swept British trade with the East Indies off the seas."[39]

During the war, the tobacco trade from Virginia and Maryland was effectively stopped (as was the sugar trade from Jamaica and Barbados) as inventory "remained idle in the colonies for want of shipping and of convoys to escort the shipping to the only lawful market in England."[40] Revenue from Virginia plantations was particularly important. As an earlier Virginia governor noted in a 1683 letter begging for the dispatch of a frigate to the colony, "the revenue of Virginia exceeds that of all the other plantations put together."[41]

Despite British attacks on French strongholds in the Caribbean (including Martinique, Guadeloupe and Hispaniola), "One and all of them had failed, with disgrace and disaster; and after huge expenditure of lives and of treasure, the peril of the French fleet remained as formidable as ever."[42]

Without the ability to trade freely with the colonies and the pressure of war-related expenses, British finances were ravaged.

Nicholson was aware of these dangers and the effects of piracy and had developed a hatred for piracy and the institutions that perpetuated the trade. He had already, as lieutenant governor of New England, proven himself to be a relentless pirate hunter and enforcer.

As governor of Maryland, Nicholson had championed his own proclamation against pirates to supplement the royal proclamation and commands from the Crown related to pirate Henry Every.[43] Nicholson admitted his feelings about pirates to the privy council:

> *I confess that I always abhorred such sort of profligate men and their barbarous actions; for sure they are the disgrace of mankind in general and of the noble, valiant, generous English in particular, who have the happiness of being governed by so great a king.*[44]

Governor Nicholson harbored general distrust for a number of the institutions involved in government and trade, including the Quakers, "whose peace principle, he feared, compromised colonial defense," as they were "vocal challenger[s] of charter and proprietary governments."[45] Nicholson believed other local governors were doing too little to suppress (or perhaps too much to encourage) piracy, and others believed he was right.

A series of letters sent by the Council of Trade and Plantations in February 1697 included the king's order that "all governors shall do their utmost to repress pirates and piracy."[46] In 1699, Robert Quary (who served as judge of the admiralty for the southern colonies, from Pennsylvania southward, and who would later become surveyor general of the customs for Maryland, New Jersey, New York, Pennsylvania and Virginia) protested, "'Not a magistrate of this country will concern himself but complains against me for disturbing the men that bring money into the country."[47]

In Connecticut, where merchants and businessmen heavily influenced the annual gubernatorial election, the governor and candidates for governor "tolerated the rovers" so as not to lose political favor from those merchants who benefited from the elicit trading.[48] A February 9, 1697 letter from the Council of Trade and Plantations to the governor and Company of Connecticut, quoted previously, was clear in its messaging to the Connecticut governor: "All governors shall do their utmost to repress pirates and piracy, *of which you will take notice.*"[49]

In Massachusetts, loose government oversight and customs controls allowed pirates who were visiting that colony to openly trade with local merchants, selling their prizes, cargoes and goods to local merchants and fitting out future expeditions. Even those pirates who were arrested for their behavior were "permitted to purchase their freedom."[50] Neighboring Rhode Island was not much different and "had become a refuge and clearinghouse for pirate booty."[51]

The government of New York, including the provinces of East and West Jersey (now part of modern-day New Jersey), was a particularly egregious offender and had changed significantly since Nicholson served as lieutenant governor of the colony.[52] Governor Benjamin Fletcher took, at best, an apathetic approach to pirates within the colony. In 1696, for example, as a known pirate ship arrived within his colony, Fletcher shrugged off the implications of having the pirates walking the streets. Governor Fletcher would write to the Lords of Trade and Plantations, providing simply that the pirates "shared their money, left their ship and separated," leaving only one man in the colony (whom Fletcher advised that he was "not to depart without leave and to live amenable to the laws").[53]

Fletcher was accused of not simply a lackadaisical attitude in customs and trade enforcement, however, but of "openly encouraging and protecting pirates."[54] There was evidence that Governor Fletcher sold protection to pirates who wanted to trade in New York at a cost of £150 per person. A "prominent member of the council was his chief broker" in negotiating these deals. In one flagrantly beneficial transaction, Fletcher was provided a vessel (which he sold for £800) in exchange for protection granted to a group of pirates.[55]

Why not, Fletcher might say, "Their treasure was Spanish money; they enrich the charter governments."[56]

Along the "lonely coasts" of East Jersey and Delaware, pirates "could careen their ships and trade freely with the natives."[57] With no forts to fend off the pirates, many could do what they wish. And it was rumored that the

"He Had Found the Captain Agreeable and Companionable," originally published in "Sea Robbers of New York," *Harper's Magazine*, November 1894. *From Wikimedia Commons*.

"Jerseys were not immediately under the authority of the king"; therefore, pirates could not "be seized or punished in that colony."[58]

As early as 1684, North Carolina had developed a reputation "by harbouring and encouraging of pirates in Carolina and other governments and proprietys where there is no law to restrain them." In 1697, the Board of Trade complained of "Carolina as too ordinary a receptacle of pyrats," a reputation which did not improve as the Board of Trade, in 1701, complained that the Carolinas "continue to be the refuge and retreat of pirates and illegal traders." Different from other colonies was the pervasiveness of pirate sympathies in the Carolinas; these sympathies were not reserved for the merchant class or politicians.

Nay, these sympathies appeared to have been shared by most Carolinians of the time. One of the more telling incidents occurred in January 1689, when the *Swift* mistakenly ran aground near Currituck Inlet.[59] The *Swift* "was beset by a horde of local inhabitants, who blatantly seized and burned papers thought to connect them with piratical activities."[60] This seemingly solidified the reputation of the Carolinas, and by the turn of the eighteenth century, the Carolinas "were reported to be rapidly becoming the principal pirate sanctuaries in the Atlantic Coast."[61] The proprietary governments of North and South Carolina had been so inattentive to the issue of piracy, the Board of Trade recommended the proprietary charters be revoked.

Maryland, where Nicholson had previously served as governor, was seen as an unreliable partner in the struggle against piracy (or other criminals or of "strange Indians"). In one letter from Governor Nicholson to his successor in Maryland, Governor Nehemiah Blakiston, Nicholson warned, "It would be well, in these strange times, to take precautions against the spread of false reports and that the people on the frontiers be vigilant."[62] An apparently false accusation from Blakiston of treason caused Nicholson to rally a small militia force to the head of the Potomac for no reason.

With limited resources to protect the colony, Nicholson's patience was thin. Firing back at Blakiston, Nicholson warned the neighboring governor to mind the affairs of his own colony. Concerned that Blakiston might order Captain Rowe of the HMS *Dumbarton* to seize vessels as instructed by a Mr. George Layfield, who was appointed customs official by Patrick Mein, a surveyor (not a customs officer), and that a Mr. Abbington, "an ordinary keeper takes on him to be collector of the king's customs in Patuxent River," Nicholson castigated Blakiston so that he would "see that the acts are enforced and Their Majesties not defrauded of their dues."[63]

Of all of the colonies, however, Nicholson was most concerned about "the excesses of the Markham administration in Pennsylvania" and "Markham's piratical associates."[64] Nicholson, who had observed a steady increase in piracy and illicit trade in Pennsylvania, "frequently berated Markham for his affinity for those in that profession."[65] He advised the Crown that "that the government of Pennsylvania, as he [William Penn] now manages it, is every way prejudicial to the king's interest."[66]

Markham, who, at one time, served under New York governor Benjamin Fletcher (Fletcher served previously as the governor of Pennsylvania), shared the practice of selective protection to pirates for one hundred pounds each and "gained a reputation as a 'steddy freind' of pirates."[67]

Markham's ties to piracy were not simply based on commerce; they were familial as well. Markham's daughter, with his permission, married a notable pirate, James Brown (who had sailed with John Avery). Brown socialized among the most powerful circles in the colony, and Brown even secured a seat in the Pennsylvania assembly. Brown's legislative career was cut short, however, when the assembly voted to expel Brown after finding he was "unfit to sit here."[68]

Pennsylvania's reputation was no secret, and according to William Penn (Markham's first cousin), rumors spread through London that Pennsylvanians "not only wink att but imbrace pirats, shipps and men."[69] Among the most damning and significant testimonies came from Admiralty Judge Colonel Robert Quary to the Council of Trade and Plantations:

> The government would not so much as issue out a proclamation against the pirates, eight of whom I apprehended in spite of the inhabitants' endeavours to prevent me. The pirates committed to gaol are out upon bail; they walk the streets with their pockets full of gold and are the constant companions of the chief in the government. They threaten my life and those who were active in apprehending them; carry their prohibited goods publicly in boats from one place to another for a market; threaten the lives of the king's collectors and with force and arms rescue their goods from them. The favour which the pirates find in these governments hath been of a very fatal consequence to several of H.M. subjects, who have had their ships and goods carried out of this port by their own ships' crews; for those who never designed to do an ill thing, seeing pirates and murderers at liberty, respected and made the companions of the best and masters of such great sums of money, it encourages them to turn villains, too. The 2,000 pieces of eight which I had in my custody, the two pirates from whom I took it, since they

are bailed, resolve to bring their action against me for it, being encouraged thereto by this government. I am sure they will recover against me, so that if I cannot delay the business till I hear from you, I must return them the money. And though I have disbursed considerable of my own money in seizing them, I shall not be allowed one penny. They resolve to bring these pirates to a trial, though there is not so much as an act passed in the Jerseys for the trial of piracy, nor is there in either government any evidence for the king, as they have managed it. However, the force of gold will do anything. All these parts swarm with pirates so that if some speedy and effectual course be not taken, the trade of America will be ruined.[70]

This reputation continued even after Penn relieved Markham of the duties of his office. According to author Hugh Rankin, in a 1703 pamphlet, "These Quaker[s] have a neat way of getting money by encouraging the pyrates, when they bring in a good store of gold, so that when [John] Avery's men were here in 1697, the Quaking justices were for letting them live quietly, or else they were bailed easily."[71]

Markham would snap back at Nicholson, however, quipping that "Nicholson habitually discovered 'pirates' in nearly every colony except his own."[72] Nicholson, perhaps, according to Markham, was looking to wrest control of Pennsylvania for himself.[73]

Without significant vigilance and intervention from the government, Virginia could easily have followed its neighbors, the Carolinas, New York (including East and West Jersey) and Delaware, in allowing pirates and smugglers to take advantage of its geography. By that time, however, Nicholson had demonstrated a willingness to support—both verbally and monetarily—colonial enforcement officials.[74]

4

"HUES AND CRYES WERE RAISED THROUGHOUT THE COLONY"

In the spring of 1699, Virginia's settlements were still centered on the creeks, rivers and bays that fed into the Chesapeake Bay and the Sea of Virginia (now the Atlantic Ocean).

The creeks, rivers and bays of these areas were already being used by smugglers to avoid paying duties on their goods by evading customs officials, and they would, very soon, be increasingly used by pirates and buccaneers. As described by author Lloyd Haynes Williams, "Smuggling was easy, since vessels could and did slip by without paying proper duty as required. Pirates could swoop down on the unsuspecting colony and plunder shipping along the bays in rivers and even plantations along shore."[75]

Virginia, comprised completely of the areas within modern-day Hampton Roads, had a population of almost eighty thousand living in twenty-three counties, making it the largest among the American colonies.[76] Counties of Virginia at that time included familiar names like James City, New Kent, Charles City and Henrico (on what locals now refer to as the "Peninsula"), which includes the land between the York and James Rivers, Princess Anne (now part of the city of Virginia Beach), Norfolk, Nansemond (included now in the city of Suffolk) and Isle of Wight, as well as Accomac and Northampton on Virginia's Eastern Shore.[77]

Although Jamestown was well established, Virginia was "in so ill a condition both by…sea and land frontiers."[78] Princess Anne County was "pretty large and the Inhabitants dispersed" and, like most of the other counties in Virginia, was "badly armed." Norfolk, which had only recently been established, was in similar condition.[79] Elizabeth City County was "one

Nova Virginiae tabula, Hendrik Hondius, cartographer, 1642. *Courtesy of the Library of Congress, Geography and Map Division.*

of the most likely counties for an enemy to land in," and the militia was "badly armed."[80]

On June 22, 1688, Captain Simon Rowe of the frigate *Dunbarton* was patrolling the area near the mouth of the James and Elizabeth Rivers. During an otherwise routine stop of a shallop sailed by local resident Charles Boult, a junior officer noticed a large chest being transported by John Hinson, Edward Davis and Lionel Wafer (author of *A New Voyage and Description of the Isthmus of America*).[81] All three men had sailed with William Dampier as he circumnavigated the globe and were obviously, from their appearance, not English or Virginian gentlemen.

The contents of the chest must have left Rowe immediately speechless. Within the chest were:

> *Thirty-seven silver plates…ten bullets conceived to be melted silver…some fowle lynnen* [foul linen]*…remnants of silke…three baggs of Spanish money marked "LW" conteyning 1,100 dollars or there abouts…two baggs of spanish money…about 800 peeces of eight.*[82]

Rowe immediately had Hinson, Davis and Wafer placed in irons and notified the governor by letter of the capture of these obvious pirates.

After several years of legal wrangling, the pirates enlisted the legal services (and influence) of an attorney, Micajah Perry, filing petitions in Virginia and London to recover the chests and their contents. Eventually, the three pirates traveled to London on a petition to the monarchy.

Reverend James Blair was in London at the same time as Hinson, Davis and Wafer for his "college business," which, for a variety of reasons, had been consistently delayed.[83] Ultimately, however, Blair was successful in securing funds for the new college.

First, a Mr. Boyle died while Blair was in London and "left a considerable legacy for pious uses."[84] Using his relationship with the Bishop of Salisbury, Blair was able to convince Boyle's executors to contribute £200 "for our college."[85]

Then, Blair became involved with Hinson, Davis and Wafer, who had "been long kept in suspense about that money which Captain Roe seized in Virginia." Apparently, according to Blair, the pirate's friends had become "tired [of] interceeding for them, and no money was like to come at last."[86]

Blair saw this as an opportunity and personally

> undertook to get them their money provided they would give a considerable share of it to our Virginia College. They engaged to give 300 pounds, and I presently employed the Archbishop of Canterbury and Bishop of London, who have so managed it with the council that the council is very glad of the expedient, and I am assured it will take effect. This day, their petition was read before a committee for plantations, and I subscribed it, signifying that the petitioners had devoted £300 of the money towards the carrying on the design of a college in Virginia if they might have an order for the rest, and the thing would have past but yet the Lords thought they offered too little money; so I am desired to try if I can bring them up to £500. So yet tho' my main business is not yet finished yet, I make use of my time for something else than mere waiting. But I confess, the trouble of managing the affair is so vastly great beyond expectation, that I doubt, could I have foreseen it, I should never have had the courage to have undertaken it.[87]

On February 8, 1693, with a combination of funds that included the £300 pledged by the pirates, the College of William and Mary in Williamsburg, Virginia, was established.

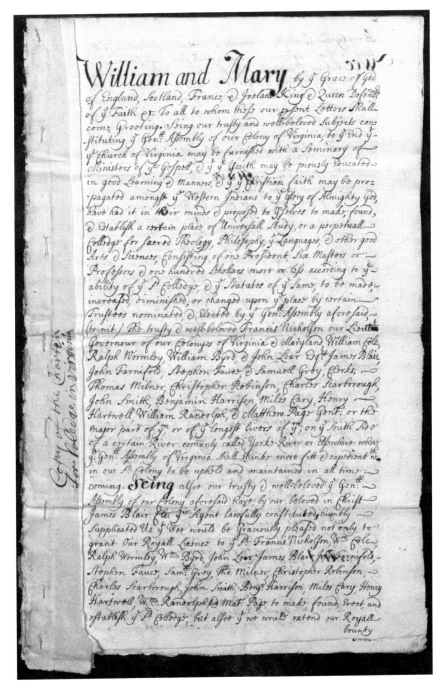

College of William and Mary royal charter, 1693. *Courtesy of Royal Charter Collection, Special Collections Research Center, Earl Gregg Swem Library, College of William and Mary.*

While Hinson, Davis and Wafer were confined (in Virginia and in England), the HMS *Dumbarton* kept the Chesapeake Bay and its rivers and tributaries "relatively free from piratical invasions."[88] In 1691, however, the HMS *Dumbarton* succumbed to shipworms and wear and tear and was beached and scrapped for wood and parts (its cannons mounted at Tindall's Point and its sails and riggings kept as replacements for other ships).[89]

The arrival of Hinson, Davis and Wafer was not Virginia's first exposure to pirates. Governor William Berkeley, Virginia's longest-serving governor, described Virginia's waters in the 1660s as being "so full of pirates that it is almost impossible for any ship to go home and safety."[90]

Several decades later, under then governor Thomas Culpeper (the second Baron Culpeper of Thoresway), Virginia experienced one of its first instances of piracy of any significance. During that summer, a ship came into the Chesapeake Bay through the Virginia capes and dropped anchor at the mouth of the York River. The pirate crew entered small boats and made their way up the river to Tindall's Point (across from what is now known as Yorktown). When they arrived, the pirates entered and plundered two different houses, carrying away a considerable number of goods, money and silverplate.

The piracy greatly alarmed the Council of Virginia. The government, in an effort to prevent what it expected to be continued piracy along the Chesapeake Bay and its tributaries, established plans for capturing the sea rovers.

Colonel William Cole impressed a private ship, either a pink bark or ketch, with enough rigging and tackle to prepare for a chase. He also gathered a number of men, twelve barrels of pork and other provisions for a voyage to chase the pirates.

The pirates were eventually caught in Rhode Island, and five were returned to Virginia with the stolen goods from the two homes. The men were kept in the Middlesex County Gaol to await trial. The five men, however, escaped; two of the pirates were eventually captured, but the three others disappeared.

The remaining men were tried on charges of piracy, convicted and sentenced to be hanged by the neck until dead. On the night before their execution, the two pirates successfully petitioned the governor for a two-day reprieve from the execution so that one of the men could be baptized. During those two days before execution, however, the men again escaped by removing two iron bars from the jail windows.

"Hues and cryes" were raised throughout the colony, as the captives were on the loose. Three days later, the two men voluntarily returned to the prison, sneaking in the same way they had snuck out. They had accomplished their desires, having prepared themselves for death.[91]

The inhabitants of Jamestown were so impressed by the honesty of the two prisoners they petitioned the governor to pardon the men. The Lords of Trade and Plantations agreed, and Governor Howard was later to pardon the men with the assurance that they would not return to piracy.

By July 1683, according to acting governor Nicholas Spencer:

> *All is quiet* [, but]*…in this year and last this Government has been much infested by privateers, or rather pirates, of whom we have great apprehensions, for our nakedness lays us open to their outrages while the Government is wholly unable to provide adequate means of defence. Lord Culpeper, however, fitted and entered into the King's service a small vessel of eighteen men and officers to cruise within the bay. This of course can do little more than give us timely notice of an intended attack*[.][92]

Nicholas Spencer continued on in his letter, expressing anxiety that "the King would graciously send us a small man-of-war," and begging Sir Leoline Jenkins for his "good offices" and assistance.[93]

Virginia's primary protection against these smugglers was the sixteen-gun sloop the HMS *Essex Prize*, which only a few months prior to Nicholson's installment as governor replaced the thirty-two-gun fifth-rate HMS *Dover Prize*. The new guardian ship the *Essex Prize* was "of considerably lesser force" than the *Dover Prize* and was commanded by Captain Jon Aldred, known to have "somewhat-less-than-aggressive tendencies."[94]

Aldred's tendencies may not have created significant issues under the ailing former governor Sir Edmund Andros, but they certainly "strained" his relationship with "the aggressive enemy of all pirates, Francis Nicholson," with whom he would have "to orchestrate his activities for the best interests of Virginia."[95]

When Nicholson first arrived in Virginia in May 1690, Nicholson found Virginians generally "in alarm at news of great depredations made by the French and Indians in New England and New York."[96] His focus on empowering the local militia and securing access to Virginia was obvious. Nicholson set out immediately to "view the heads of the rivers that lie exposed to these enemies and to examine the condition of the militia."[97]

The militia was "neither so well armed nor so well disciplined as present circumstances require," and Virginia's "upper plantations are remote and very open to attack."[98] Nicholson knew something must be done. Although

Nicholson expressed a "wish [that] an order could be sent to forbid more out plantations. In case of war with the Indians, those settlers must retire lower down or run great risk of being cut off."[99]

Nicholson would tour "some of the places which are called forts," but he did "not think they deserve the name."[100] An aggressive executive, Nicholson would not accept the current state of defense, expressing his intent to the Lords of Trade and Plantations "by next ship to report further" on the defensive fortification "and on the militia," which Nicholson was doing his "best to set in order."[101]

In addition to the land fortifications, Nicholson found insufficient maritime defenses. Meeting with Captain Simon Rowe of the HMS *Dumbarton* (twenty guns), Nicholson discovered that the captain was "in want of powder and gunners' stores" and provided what was available for that purpose.[102]

Despite his efforts, Nicholson was unable to completely secure Virginia's borders and "was undoubtedly frustrated with the inability to keep a man of war constantly cruising about the bay."[103]

The January 27, 1692 minutes of the Council of Virginia made it clear the colony remained, at that time, years after Nicholson took office, in a "defenceless condition" and the council asked "the king to send us a fireship in lieu of arms."[104] If something wasn't done, Nicholson knew that pirates and smugglers would continue to use the unprotected backwater tributaries along Virginia's Eastern Shore in particular.

By April 1692, Governor Nicholson had met with the four burgesses representing Northampton and Accomac Counties who were in Jamestown and the council to study whether a policy that allowed "noe ships or vessells whatsoever…be permitted to goe into the little rivers and harbours on the seaboardside of the Eastern Shore," an area "enemyes and falce traders" would regularly frequent.[105] Ultimately, the burgesses declared that such a policy would not be harmful, and the council prohibited all ships from using any of the rivers or harbors on the Atlantic side of Virginia's Eastern Shore.[106]

Northampton and Accomac Counties were tasked with monitoring the coast in a way "to prevent any mischief that may happen by the suddain arrival of an enemy from sea."[107] Princess Anne County (now modern-day Virginia Beach) would begin maintaining a lookout (named Adam Hays) on the Atlantic coast, paid for by the Virginia General Assembly.[108]

With Nicholson's heightened sensitivity to the security of Virginia's outlying areas and maritime frontiers, he was one of the first colonial governors to observe the return of pirates coming from the Red Sea.[109] In July 1692, Nicholson advised the Lords of Trade and Plantations:

I have an account that a ship lately came to South Carolina, which pretended to have come from the Red Sea and to have captured a Moorish ship, which brought £2,000 a piece to the hundred men of the crew. They parted in Carolina, and I hear that several of them are in Pennsylvania, where the government, owing to the Quakers falling out among themselves, is very loose. I beg your orders for my guidance, in case any of these men should come here, for it such people be encouraged they will debauch the inhabitants and make them leave planting to follow the same trade. I very much fear that these sort of privateers, or rather pirates, when they have lavishly spent what they unjustly get, are ready to make a disturbance.[110]

Later, in 1695, Nicholson (then the governor of Maryland) expressed his concern about the encouragement of illegal trade by the Quakers and its impact on the settling of pirates in Maryland.

Nicholson would express significant concern about the money flowing into the colony from illegal trade, recognizing how enticing the large amounts of cash could be on those within the colony. The governor would complain to the Duke of Shrewsbery:

I thought it my duty to report this, as also how the illegal trade is managed there, which, unless speedily prevented, may be prejudicial to the king's revenue. They [the Quakers] *send tobacco to Scotland (having many Scotchmen living and trading among them) and to other unlawful places in Europe, as also to Curaçoa and Surinam, whither they cunningly convey their tobacco in casks, with flour or bread at each end. They contrive to be there when the Dutch Europe fleet comes, that they may have their goods, which are sold as cheap in Pennsylvania as in Holland. Pirates have been leaving that country of late, who, coming from the Red Sea bring in £1,000 or £1,500 a man. From thence, they set out again and easily entice seamen to leave the ships in these parts, which is very prejudicial to trade. I fear one or two ships will be left behind in this province by reason of their men running away, though I have used all possible means to prevent them, but the country is so open that it is almost impossible to hinder them. I do not doubt that at least a hundred men have run thither from the Virginia and Maryland fleet, for they are now building twelve or fourteen sloops, brigantines and other vessels in order to manage their trade.*[111]

Nicholson's military experience and severe application of the rule of law to trade and the treatment of piracy engendered a specific reputation for the governor. Nicholson, as would be reported in a May 1698 letter, "is really zealous to suppress piracy and illegal trade and was formerly very severe to those who were even suspected of countenancing pirates so that not one of [Henry] Every's men came to Maryland."[112]

5

"I AM KIDD"

By the spring of 1699, Nicholson was again in full control of the Virginia colony. Renewing his prior focus of securing Virginia's shorelines was already a priority when Nicholson received additional orders from the lords of justice of England in 1699.[113] Nicholson and the Council of Virginia were alerted to the possible presence of Captain William Kidd and his ship the *Adventure Galley* in Virginia waters.

Nicholson and the other "respective governors of the collony under His Maj's obedience in America" were given "strict orders" to "take particular care for apprehending the said Kidd and his accomplices whenever he or they shall arive in any of the said plantation."[114] Upon capture, the lord justices of England directed that Kidd "and his assoceates be prosecuted with the utmost rigour of law."[115] America, including Virginia and its pirate-hating governor Francis Nicholson, was on high alert.

Captain Kidd, once a pirate-hunter himself, gained infamy by plundering French, Moorish, Portuguese and Armenian ships (one of which, the *Quedagh Merchant*, was rumored to have been in the employ of the East India Company, "which complained loudly about Kidd's activities to British authorities").[116]

In July 1699, the ship *Providence Galley* was sailing toward the Virginia Capes and the Chesapeake Bay.[117] Earlier in the year, the captain of the *Providence Galley*, John James, had taken control of the ship through a mutiny, marooning the original Dutch captain and fifteen others on one of the Berry Islands in the Bahamas.[118]

Captain John James, "a Welshman of Glamorganshire," like many of his brethren of the sea, bore both the scars of battle and blemishes left by disease.[119] James joined a list of ugly, disfigured men terrorizing the Virginia coast. Vivid descriptions of these disfigurements and bodily oddities would help frame a narrative of fear and distrust among merchants and common citizens who might otherwise trade or fraternize with the "brethren of the coast."

Francis Nicholson would describe other "notorious pyrates" as:

> *Of ordinary stature, rawboned, very pale complexion, dark hair, remarkably deformed by an attraction of the lower eyelid, about thirty years of age.*

> *Tall, lusty rawboned, long visage, swarthy, about twenty-eight years of age.*

> *Short and small Black, much squint-eyed, about ten years of age.*

> *Short, very well sett, fresh-coloured, pock-fretten, about twenty years of age.*

> *Short, very small Black, blind of one eye, about eighteen years of age.*

> *Tall, meagre, sickly complexion, large black eyes, about thirty years of age.*

Similarly, John James "was a man of middle stature, square-shouldered, large-jointed, lean, much disfigured with the smallpox, broad speech, thick-lipped, a blemish or cast in his left eye but courteous."[120]

According to contemporary reports, Captain James had aboard *Providence Galley* a large trove of gold and silver worth "£3,000,000 [approximately £422,500,000 or $588,204,500 in 2021] sterling in gold and silver," an extraordinary amount.[121] The captain and crew were so rich with gold, "ye company and captain himself" were observed "to have gold chains about their necks. The captain had a gold tooth picker hanging at it."[122]

Approaching Cape Henry and Cape Charles, Captain James and the *Providence Galley* easily took the small merchant vessel *Hope*, which was making its way from Virginia to London.[123] The taking of the *Hope* would have otherwise been insignificant (the pirates took only a few items), except the *Hope* was carrying six months' worth of records from the HMS *Essex Prize*.[124]

The disfigured pirate must have flicked his golden toothpick approvingly as he read the intelligence reports. According to the reports, Maryland and Virginia had significant weaknesses in their maritime defense. The reports

Ships in Close Combat in Harbor, illustration in *De Americaensche Zee-Roovers*, A.O. Exquemelin photograph. *Courtesy of the Library of Congress.*

also confirmed that sixteen-gun sloop the HMS *Essex Prize* was the only protection for the waters of the Chesapeake.[125] Through his interrogation of the *Hope*'s crew, James also knew of the "infirmities" of the *Essex Prize*, including "its size, weakness and possibly even the somewhat temperamental nature of her captain."[126] James and his crew decided they would take this opportunity head-on and engage the HMS *Essex Prize* directly.

On the morning of July 25, 1699, the crew of the HMS *Essex Prize* and the ship itself were beaten up and exhausted from a "brutal" storm the night before.[127] That night, as things normalized about the *Essex Prize* from the storm, Captain Aldred had it anchored a few miles from Cape Henry. While at anchor, a small flyboat, the *Maryland Merchant*, was spotted outward-bound from Virginia to Bristol.

James and his crew had also taken note of the *Maryland Merchant* when it passed the Lynnhaven Bay earlier in the evening, prepared for sail and set after the *Maryland Merchant* out of the Capes of Virginia and into the Atlantic.

Aldred, having spotted James's ship coming out of the Lynnhaven and toward the *Maryland Merchant*, was immediately suspicious. The weary crew of the *Essex Prize* moved to investigate and intercept the *Providence Galley*. The *Essex Prize* was quickly within hailing distance of *Providence Galley*, but the pirates were in no mood to talk. James raised "the king's colors and a blood-red flag" before firing their "guns without shot" as a warning to Aldred's guardship.[128]

James finally recognized the *Essex Prize* for what it was and was ecstatic that Virginia's only guardship had fallen right into his hands. He would fight to seize the opportunity to permanently disable the colony's naval defense and "unloaded a vicious full broadside" on *Essex Prize*.[129]

Aldred, recognizing he was overmatched, -manned and -gunned, had no interest in engaging in a fight. James, on the other hand, was ready more than ever for a fight and "bore down" on the *Essex Prize*. Aldred's only hope was to lure the aggressive James away from the *Maryland Merchant* and into shallower waters. The *Providence Galley* was relentless in its pursuit, like "a shark in pursuit of a dolphin."[130]

Aldred and the *Essex Prize* eventually made their way into the shallows, recording in the ship's log, "I kept a leading fight to ye southward towards Cape Henry, my master being well acquainted with ye shoals."[131] James did not take the bait and instead hovered on the outskirts of the shallows. Aldred, however, continued "ghosting" the *Providence Galley* and never committed "full combat" with James.[132]

Soon thereafter, James turned his attention to the *Maryland Merchant*, which had, inexplicably, attempted to flee through the Chesapeake Bay and into the James River instead of out toward the Atlantic. James would easily take the *Maryland Merchant* while *Essex Prize* looked on, helpless. James quickly took the crew of *Maryland Merchant* aboard his own ships and left the *Maryland Merchant* unmanned and at anchor while he turned his attention back to Aldred.

Aldred continued his game of cat and mouse but failed to lure the *Providence Galley* into trouble. James eventually tired of the game and turned back to the *Maryland Merchant* and its crew. James interrogated the *Maryland Merchant*'s captain, Richard Burgess. But through his conversations with James, Burgess was able to discern additional information about Captain James and his ship, the *Providence Galley*.

"For whom is *Essex Prize* cruising?" Captain James asked.[133]

"One Captain Kidd," Burgess answered.

Captain James responded coldly, "I am Kidd."[134]

Burgess was convinced James was telling the truth, for "he was called John James by the company; but from the description I have of him in the country, he is said to be Kidd."[135] James was, of course, not Captain William Kidd, who was arrested in New York the month prior by order of Governor Bellomont, a former backer of Kidd's.[136]

William Kidd, privateer and pirate. Eighteenth-century portrait by Sir James Thornhill. *From Wikimedia Commons.*

In a seeming confirmation that James had aboard the *Providence Galley* significant wealth, James and his crew "thought it not worth their while to take a gentleman's plate and money, value nigh £100," instead leaving it on *Maryland Merchant.*[137]

Aldred and the *Essex Prize* had proven themselves insufficient to guard the harbors and waterways of Virginia. His timidity and lack of force provided little to no protection of the colony. Aldred limped back toward the Hampton Roads area to report back to Governor Nicholson about the encounter.

"Ye pirate ship, being very clean, wronged me much," wrote Aldred. Aldred excused his timidity, writing also that if he had engaged James directly, "he would have overpowered me with men."[138]

Even though he was the captain of the only significant guardship in the Chesapeake Bay, Aldred turned to Governor Nicholson for guidance and protection. Aldred "thought it more service to make sail into ye shore to acquaint ye governor thereof, to provide his [the pirate's] doing any further damage and to make a strong defence agst him."[139] Although he had his reasoning for a retreat (to warn and prevent other ships from leaving the harbor and to secure more crewmen for a potential engagement), Aldred was relieved to have survived the encounter with only minimal damage to his ship's sails and, symbolically, colors.

For pirates, like James, buccaneers, sea rovers, smugglers and freebooters, Virginia was now open for business. More than thirty ships were taken by pirates of the Chesapeake in the three months after James seized the *Maryland Merchant* and engaged the HMS *Essex Prize.*[140]

Nicholson reacted immediately to the attack on Virginia by Captain James and the *Providence Galley*, calling a meeting of the council at Jamestown. The details of the pirate invasion were "testily laid" out before the council, including letters from Captain Aldred and related documents from Colonel William Wilson (commander of the militia of Elizabeth City County).[141]

Descriptions of Captain James, the *Providence Galley*, its crew and their crimes were sent to the colonial governments of the north in an attempt to bring the men to justice.[142]

The council was sympathetic to Captain Aldred, who had accepted the fate of Virginia that "a pyrate or other enemy may land and execute his intended mischief, before any number of men can be gotten together, and put on board a ship to oppose him" and that it would be impossible to rally enough men for a warship in the event of an emergency "without going to great expense."[143]

Nicholson, however, would have none of it. Governor Nicholson's "growing animosity toward Captain Aldred, fueled by the captain's apparent timidity in battle and unwillingness to seek information about the pirates until they had departed, had reached a new height."[144] Nicholson and Aldred were "both testy men, easy to anger and wearing their vexations on their shoulders as a mantle."[145]

It was clear to Nicholson and the council that Captain Aldred and the HMS *Essex Prize* did not provide enough force protection for the colony. The council urged Governor Nicholson to request from the king a "a ship of sufficient force to defend his colony and dominion agst pyrats, and yet there may be allowed to her a small tender, which, in case of necessity, may serve as a fire ship."[146]

In addition to the request for additional firepower at sea, Governor Nicholson issued several orders to militia commanders in Norfolk, Princess Anne, Accomac, Northampton and Elizabeth City to appoint sentinels to watch and patrol the coast until late fall (September 29), when changing weather conditions made it less likely for pirates to carry on activities in the Chesapeake Bay, Virginia capes and contributing waters.[147] Nicholson demanded Virginia's borders to the sea be secured.

Nicholson's frustration with Aldred's inability to deter "seaborne brigandry" continued throughout the fall, when a pirate, Henry King (originally a trader from Pennsylvania), seized the London merchantman *John Hopewell*, commanded by Captain Henry Munday, off the coast of Virginia. A letter dated November 1699 was sent by the owners of the ship to Governor Nicholson with a list of names of the nine deserters (who joined the pirate crew), demanding that if the deserters ever landed again in Virginia, Nicholson should require their apprehension and bring them to trial.[148]

Except for the coming of winter, which brought seasonal relief from piracy along the Mid-Atlantic colonies while the rovers sailed south to the West Indies, Caribbean and Gulf of Mexico, Nicholson's government was powerless to stop the scourge of piracy. Nicholson would be able to focus his attention on other pressing matters of government, including the "enforcement of laws against fornication, laws against blasphemy, laws to restrain tippling houses and laws about servants impregnated by their masters."[149]

6

"MOST EXPEDIENT MANNER FOR TRYING PIRATES"

John James in Virginia was one of many pirates "infesting those coasts" in "His Majesty's plantations in America."[150] In order for the colonial governors to exact an appropriate and more uniform punishment of pirates, the governors were ordered by the king to:

> *Send hither in safe custody all the pirates who are now in prison or shall or may be at the time of their receiving those directions, together with the evidences upon which they have been seized and which may be of any use towards their convictions here; and that they take care to secure their goods and effects, to be disposed of as shall be determined by law.*[151]

The king's order did not consider, apparently, the expense and risk associated with detaining pirates or, in some cases, entire pirate crews, through entire voyages across the Atlantic to London. This risk was heightened by the nature of the pirates, men who had made a practice (and living) of violently overtaking ships at sea.

Certain more reliable governors, including Sir William Beeston (the governor of Jamaica), Colonel Christopher Codrington (the governor of the Leeward Islands), Francis Nicholson, Nathaniel Blakiston (the governor of Maryland) and Richard, Earl of Bellomont (the governor of Massachusetts Bay, New York and New Hampshire) were granted discretion to determine the "most expedient" manner for trying pirates, whether it be in their colonies or in London.[152]

Directives to the other colonies, including to the governors of Pennsylvania (William Penn), Connecticut and Rhode Island, to those "such as are in the present in execution of the government of East and West New Jersey," the lords proprietors of Carolina and to the lieutenant governor of Bermuda (Samuel Day) were to send pirates to England as a "standing rule" and without discretion.[153]

These instructions were in addition to acts that several colonies, most notably Jamaica, took to suppress piracy. But these acts did not garner complete support from colonial administrators. Seeing the need to do something to stymie piracy in the colonies and, "having in view the refractoriness of New England and other plantations," Parliament passed an act for the suppression of piracy, extending to "all the plantations and other foreign parts" controlled by the Crown.[154]

7

"THE OCCUPATIONS OF COW-KILLING AND CRUISING"

Throughout the 1600s, the struggle of dominion over the Caribbean between the English, Spanish and French played out on the tiny island of Tortuga, located just north of Hispaniola (what is now modern-day Haiti and the Dominican Republic).

In the 1660s, a group of "ruffians" assisted the French in regaining Tortuga from the Spanish and English. These "ruffians" were to become known as buccaneers. Although the terms are used interchangeably now, *buccaneer* and *pirate* referred to distinct groups of rough men (and the occasional woman) throughout the 1600s and early 1700s.

When the Spaniards settled in the West Indies, they set "beeves [cattle] and hogs a shore on every island they espied, which increased mightily and those places where they have a constant summer, and the grass alwayes plentiful."[155]

Hunters throughout the Caribbean, including Tortuga, sustained themselves on these cattle and pigs (as well as fish and the occasional manatee), employing indigenous methods for preserving the meat over time. The flesh of the cattle killed by the hunters was cured to preserve it to be eaten later. The method of preservation was learned from the indigenous Caribe tribesman (possibly Arawaks). The meat was laid to be dried on a wooden grate or hurdle (*grille de bois*), which the tribesmen called *barbecu*, and placed a good distance over a slow fire.

The meat, when cured, was called *boucan*, and the same name was given to the place of their cookery. The flesh of wild hogs (and sometimes the cattle,

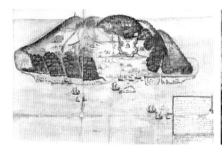 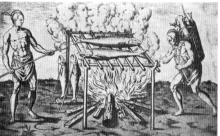

Left: Drawing of Tortuga Island during the "Brother of the Coast" period, circa the seventeenth century. *From Wikimedia Commons.*

Right: *Natives Cooking Fish. From the John White drawings in Ashe's History of North Carolina in "Letter from the Secretary of the Interior, Transmitting, in Response to a Senate Resolution of June 30, 1914, a Report on the Condition and Tribal Rights of the Indians of Robeson and Adjoining Counties of North Carolina," 1914.*

when it was intended to be kept for a length of time) was salted before it was smoked and slowly cooked on the boucan.

Some hunters sold their smoked meat to be taken aboard ships, first removing the bones, cutting the meat into convenient pieces and salting it before putting it on the boucan the next day. If kept dry, the boucan would last for six months or more (with, admittedly, a significant loss of flavor, particularly among the beef boucan).

From adopting the boucan of the indigenous tribesman, the ruffian hunters in Hispaniola came to be called *boucaniers*, later anglicized in writing by Captain William Dampier to *buccaneers*.[156]

Ships from all parts of the West Indies frequented Tortuga, leaving sailors to live and hunt on the island and picking up the buccaneer landsmen for sea voyages. Each of these men "combined in himself the occupations of cow-killing and cruising, varying the monotony of the one by occasionally trying his hand at the other."[157] The two occupations of hunting and cruising became so common that *buccaneer* was later used more often to describe those sea-roving pirates more than the land-based hunters.[158]

In any case, these men "were willing at least to lend a hand in an occasional foray against their Spanish neighbours" and "lived at constant enmity with the Spaniards."[159]

There are a number of significant, firsthand accounts of buccaneer culture. The most famous is *De Americaensche Zee-Rovers* (the *Buccaneers of America*), an eyewitness account of buccaneer life written by French surgeon turned buccaneer Alexander Exquemelin, first published in 1678. This first edition "was received with such general applause of most people, but more

Left: William Dampier portrait, holding his book, circa 1697–98. *From Wikimedia Commons.*

Right: The title page of *Historie de Boecaniers of Vreybuyters van America with Vignettes of Pirate Scenes*, 1700. *Courtesy of the Library of Congress.*

especially of the learned, as to encourage…[Exquemelin] onwards obliging the public" with a second edition.[160]

Buccaneers of America recounts the exploits of many of these rovers, detailing the French presence in Hispaniola, describing the landscape and inhabitants of the island and depicting their way of life, subculture and rules of conduct.

The study of buccaneers and other pirates of the Golden Age of Piracy can be frustrating to historians and enthusiasts. Most buccaneers and pirates were illiterate (aside from the rare case of pirates like Exquemelin or the "Gentleman Pirate" Stede Bonnet), lived outside of confines of "civilized" society, lived short lives and did not have the benefit of the comforts of a safe, secure world.[161]

Buccaneers of America is a unique resource, providing a contemporaneous, firsthand account from an "insider" of the buccaneer community. Combined with letters from governors, ship captains and other colonial and English officials and secondhand sources, much of the buccaneer lifestyle and customs have been preserved. It stands among the most influential "pirate books" of all time, along with *A General History of the Robberies and Murders of the Most Notorious Pyrates* and *The Pirates' Own Book.*

Illustration of Captain William Kidd overseeing a treasure burial, by Howard Pyle. *From Howard Pyle and Merle De Vore Johnson, eds.,* Book of Pirates: Fiction, Fact & Fancy Concerning the Buccaneers & Marooners of the Spanish Main *(New York: Harper and Brothers, 1921), Wikimedia Commons.*

Some have criticized *Buccaneers of America* and other early buccaneer histories as:

> *Boastful compositions, which have delighted in exaggeration; and what is most mischievous, they have lavished commendation on acts which demanded reprobation and have endeavoured to raise miscreants, notorious for their want of humanity, to the rank of heroes, lessening thereby the stain upon robbery, and the abhorrence naturally conceived against cruelty.*[162]

Yet "modern historians judge it to be largely accurate in its descriptions."[163]

8

"ENGAGED WITH THEM AS THEIR CAPTAIN"

In 1699, *buccaneer* was still used to refer specifically to the rugged hunters of Hispaniola. Among those hunters was Louis Guittar. Born around 1667 in Brittany (France's northwesternmost region, a hilly peninsula extending out toward the Atlantic Ocean), Louis Guittar was a true buccaneer, spending almost two decades in Santo Domingo in Hispaniola living off the land and hunting.[164]

As a buccaneer, Guittar may have adopted many of the customs attributed to buccaneers at the time. Buccaneers had a "propensity to make things which are extraordinary appear more so," exaggerating the situation for dramatic effect or for attention, and had among them "wilder, more restless spirits."[165]

This buccaneer spirit of exaggeration sometimes evidenced itself in the creative and brutal methods buccaneers used when torturing their captives and enemies. Their methods and practices for interrogation and torture made future pirates of the golden age look timid and demure.

When interrogating prisoners, it was the "custom" of buccaneer François l'Olonnais to instantly cut those who resisted confessions in pieces and pull out their tongues.[166] l'Olonnais was particularly brutal, however, and at one time also "drew his cutlass, and with it, cut open the breast of one of those poor Spaniards, and pulling out his heart, began to bite and gnaw it with his teeth like a ravenous wolf."[167]

In a perverse homage to the boucan, means of buccaneer torture included putting their victims to the "rack," stretching the limbs of prisoners with

François l'Olonnais from
De Americaensche Zee-Roovers,
A.O. Exquemelin, 1678.
Wikimedia Commons.

cords, beating them with sticks and other instruments; placing burning matches between the fingers of their captives; wrapping "slender cords or matches twisted about their heads till their eyes burst out"; and stretching one victim with cords, "breaking both arms behind his shoulders."[168]

Another unfortunate victim was put to the rack, which disjointed his arms, before having a cord twisted on his forehead, "which they wrung so hard that his eyes appeared as big as eggs and were ready to fall out." Unable to get the information they wanted, the buccaneers continued, hanging the man by his testicles before striking him in the body. Afterward, they cut off his nose and ears, singed his face until he could no longer speak and then forced an enslaved person to run a sword through the already lifeless body.[169]

Another prisoner was strung up only by small cords tied to his two thumbs and two big toes, and a two-hundred-pound stone was placed on his belly.[170] The buccaneers were not satisfied with simply stringing up their victim by his thumbs and toes, however, and continued to burn his face, beard and hair with kindled palm leaves before carrying him, half dead, and hanging him on one of the pillars of the local church. The hanging prisoner's life was sustained with sparing amounts of food and water until the poor Portuguese tavern-keeper agreed to raise one thousand pieces of eight in exchange for his liberty.[171]

Other tortures included hanging some by "the testicles or privy members and left till they fell to the ground, those parts being torn from the bodies," before stabbing them to death.[172] They crucified others with kindled matches between their fingers and toes or, even worse, with fires at their feet to be roasted alive.[173] And according to Exquemelin, they would, at times, drag their victims to the "rack," stretching them with cords to the point that both of the victims' arms would break behind the shoulders.[174]

Interestingly, despite their perverse and diverse methods of torture, Guittar, like some buccaneers, may have also had a "great respect…for religion and for morality."[175]

The Cruelty of Lolonois *from* The Buccaneers of America, A True Account of the Most Remarkable Assaults Committed of Lat Years upon the Coasts of the West Indies by the Buccaneers of Jamaica and Tortuga *(both English and French), John Esquemeling, 1893.*

Buccaneers acknowledged a general right of participation with others, especially as it related to the prepared meats, and prohibited "bolts, locks and every species of fastening" on doors and trunks.[176] Although this was not true with Guittar, buccaneers from respectable families customarily gave up their family name, using instead a nom de guerre (alias or assumed name). Guittar was likely slovenly dressed, wearing an unwashed shirt and pantaloons dyed with animal blood.[177] Guittar's wardrobe would have been finished off with a

> belt of undressed bull's hide bound the shirt and supported on one side three or four large knives, on the other, a pouch for powder and shot. A cap with a short, pointed brim extending over the eyes, rude shoes of cowhide or pigskin made all of one piece bound over the foot, and a short, large-bore musket, completed the hunter's grotesque outfit. Often, he carried wound about his waist a sack of netting into which he crawled at night to keep off the pestiferous mosquitoes.[178]

The Buccaneer was a Picturesque Fellow, Howard Pyle. *From Howard Pyle and Merle De Vore Johnson, eds.*, Book of Pirates: Fiction, Fact & Fancy Concerning the Buccaneers & Marooners of the Spanish Main *(New York: Harper and Brothers, 1921), Wikimedia Commons.*

Like other buccaneers, Guittar would have

roamed the woods by day with his dog and apprentices, and at night, slept in the open air or in a rude shed hastily constructed of leaves and skins, which served as a house and which he called after the Indian name, "ajoupa" or "barbacoa."[179]

As a buccaneer, Guittar would have grown accustomed to living with little leftover money (living, in modern terms, "paycheck to paycheck"). After a hunt was over and the spoils divided, the men would sail to the mainland to trade for guns, powder and shot and other necessaries for another expedition. With necessities in hand, the men would use any leftover gains to give themselves

all manner of vices and debauchery, particularly to drunkenness, which they practise mostly with brandy: this they drink as liberally as the Spaniards do water. Sometimes, they buy together a pipe of wine; this they stave at one end and never cease drinking till it is out. Thus, sottishly, they live till they have no money left.

Buccaneers were not known for kindness to others, and Guittar may have been "very cruel and tyrannical to their servants (slaves)."[180]

Guittar, like other buccaneer bachelors with no wife or children, may have also participated in the *matelotage*, a noncompulsory form of civil union. In the matelotage (a derivative of the middle French word *matelot*, meaning "sailor," and from which the pirate-speak "mate" or "matey" may have been derived), a buccaneer had a "chosen and declared comrade, between whom property was in common," including plunder, food and women.[181] If one mate died, the surviving comrade inherited all of his property. For most, these unions were more fraternal or economic than lustful or loving (although certain matelotages could have included sexual or romantic relationships).

Things would change for Guittar, however, in December 1699, when a crew of pirates captured him while he was traveling to visit a friend.[182] Like many men, Guittar did not seek out piracy. Instead, piracy found Guittar. Known by reputation as being among the most capable buccaneers on the island, the pirates targeted Guittar specifically, "knew who he was, and 'they wanted a captaine and would make him theirs.'"[183]

According to Guittar, in December 1699, "he was living at Petit Gaove [Petit-Goâve, now in modern Haiti], where took a canoe, which he served to

A Buccaneer, Alfred R. Waud, artist, circa 1861–65. *Courtesy of the Library of Congress, Prints and Photographs Division.*

The Sacking of Panama, Howard Pyle. *From Howard Pyle and Merle De Vore Johnson, eds.*, Book of Pirates: Fiction, Fact & Fancy Concerning the Buccaneers & Marooners of the Spanish Main *(New York: Harper and Brothers, 1921), Wikimedia Commons.*

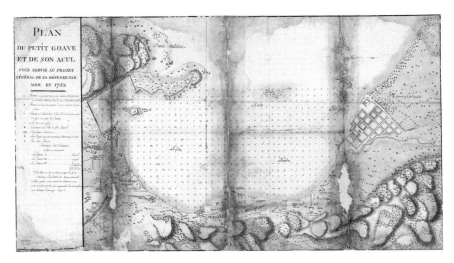

Plan du Petit Goâve et de son acul pour servir au projet général de sa défense par mer en 1752. *Courtesy of the Library of Congress, Geography and Map Division.*

go see a friend 6 or 7 leagues off."[184] As Guittar "was coming downe a little river, these men that were the pyrates sent another canoe to him, they being in a sloop, and told him he must come on board."[185] Guittar resisted initially, "and at last, they forced him being unwilling."[186]

Despite Guittar's initial resistance, "When he was on board, they told him they wanted a captaine and would make him theirs, so would not let him go, but stowed his canoe and kept him on board and then he came engaged with them" as their captain.[187]

9

"YOU MAY HAVE SEVEN OR EIGHT POUNDS A MONTH, IF YOU CAN TAKE IT"

It did not take Guittar long to take his first prize as captain of the pirates. "Ten or twelve daies after" after Guittar became captain of the small sloop, he and the crew were "sayling norwards towards the coast of St. Domingo."[188] On their way, "they mett with a little Dutch shipp [from Brazil that] designed [meaning "intended"] to go trade with or among the Spaniards." The buccaneers took some of the ship's cargo (Guittar would later say "she was loaden chiefly") and turned it away.[189]

In addition to taking cargo from the Dutch ship, Guittar also "took out of it a Dutch surgeon," impressing the surgeon and his servant, Albert L'Abbe, into the pirates' ranks.[190] The surgeon was immediately helpful, providing intelligence about a nearby "excellent, curious saylor," *The Peace*, which was headed from Surinam.[191] The surgeon was motivated to share the information to Guittar and crew "in spight [spite] to be revenged upon the master of the shipp who had wronged him of 6 or 700 crownes."[192]

The surgeon's intelligence was sound, and Guittar found *The Peace* off the island of Tortuga, capturing it with no significant altercation. Guittar swapped vessels, allowing the master to go free on Guittar's old boat.[193] The buccaneers renamed *The Peace* in their native French, and it was then known as *La Paix*, a solid fourteen-gun swift ship of Dutch construction, measuring eighty-four by twenty-five feet.[194] It was a significant upgrade for Guittar and his men.[195]

After Guittar took *La Paix*, he "intended [to go to] Martinco [Martinique]." *La Paix* would run into difficulties, however, and "in sayling

Cover of *Blackbeard, Buccaneer*, by Ralph Paine. *Blackbeard and His Crew Boards a Ship*, 1922. *From Wikimedia Commons.*

thither, their main yard broak [broke]."[196] With their ship damaged, the buccaneers would make their way toward "Carthagena" (Cartagena in modern-day Colombia), where the pirates would continue to prey on Dutch and Spanish trade routes. Outside Cartagena, Guittar "mett against a little Dutch man, a brigantine, whom he took" "without fighting," plundering and taking "only provisions out of him."[197]

With the additional speed and firepower afforded by *La Paix*, the buccaneers continued to prey on Dutch vessels. Following a brief gun

Buccaneers, Frederick Judd Waugh, artist, circa 1910. *Courtesy of the Library of Congress, Prints and Photographs Division.*

battle with a twelve-gun ship on January 9, 1700, its thirty-plus crew members "at last yielded" and were granted quarter by Guittar.[198] From the ship, Guittar plundered "4 or 500 small barrells of brandy…their best guns" and another six or seven crewmen (all Dutchmen).[199] Guittar would be clear in his recounting of the encounter that "no murther [murder] committed, only two men killed in the fight, none he saies were killed in cold blood."[200] The remaining crew were allowed to "go their own way" aboard their ship.[201]

Guittar's spree continued through the West Indies. He sailed *La Paix* from Cartagena to "Hisponiola and St. Domingo, and there mett with a little sloop and took two men out of her. They were tradesman, one was willing to go along with them, the other not, but afterwards became willing."[202]

With Guittar's early success as a captain, his reputation and crew began to grow. Thirty-eight men from another pirate ship (almost half of the 80 men aboard that ship) joined *La Paix*. Guittar would continue to add men to his crew from nearby islands, including Soi Mondy and 19 others who had been shipwrecked and "reached a rock" until "rescued" by Guittar and *La Paix*.[203] Guittar's crew eventually numbered 125 men.[204] From one ship, bound from Jamaica to Boston, the buccaneers took one hundred pounds before releasing it.

From the West Indies, *La Paix* sailed north along the colonial American seaboard. The buccaneers continued to seek out prizes. John Trimingham, the master of a brigantine sailing from the Bay of Campeche to New York, reported to the Earl of Bellomont that he "saw three Bermuda sloops taken by a pyrat," which may have been Guittar. Trimingham's report supposed the Earl of Bellomont would order frigates to pursue the pirates; it warned, however, that "if the sixth-rate frigate meets the pyrats, she will run a hazard of being taken, for I hear she is but weakly man'd."[205]

On April 17, 1700, *La Paix* captured the pink *Baltimore*, a small boat with a narrow stern, bulging sides and a flattish bottom.[206] Flying Dutch colors and feigning that *La Paix* was in distress, Guittar lured the *Baltimore* close, where he hailed the ship. According to one sailor aboard the *Baltimore*, Edmund Ashfold, "We told from whence we came and whither bound." *La Paix* then "fired a great shott" at the *Baltimore* and killed one of the merchants aboard, James Waters.[207]

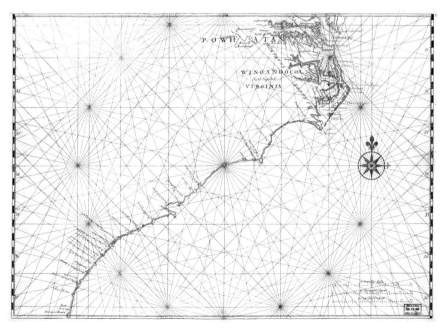

Map of Atlantic Coast of North America from the Chesapeake Bay to Florida, circa 1639. *Courtesy of the Library of Congress, Geography and Map Division.*

A small pink close hauled in a strong breeze off a rocky shore, circa 1702. *From Wikimedia Commons.*

Guittar and the pirates "carried our master and several other of our men on board their shipp" and placed a cadre of approximately eighteen to twenty men, including his quartermaster aboard.[208] Among them was *La Paix*'s pilot, John Hoogling, who mocked the sailors aboard the *Baltimore* (presumably to get the men to go along with the pirates): "You sayle in merchantmen for twenty-five shill a month and here you may have seven or eight pounds a month, if you can take it."[209]

The pirates gave orders to the pink's master, John Lovejoy, and "commanded them to sayle for the [Virginia] Capes" several hundred miles away.[210]

The small flotilla was making its way toward the Virginia Capes when, on April 23, it observed the sails of *Barbados Merchant*, a 150-ton ship bound for Virginia from Liverpool on the horizon about thirty leagues from the Virginia Capes.[211] Guittar gave chase aboard *La Paix* while his quartermaster followed in the pink. The smaller pink, unencumbered by "heavy armaments," passed *La Paix* and captured the 150-ton ship.[212]

The pirates were friendly to *Barbados Merchant*'s captain, William Fletcher, and his crew and "used much kindness to his men and persuaded them to goe with them" and sign their articles.[213] According to Captain Fletcher, the pirates were "designing to get some good ships and more company as they could," as they invited the sailors to join their crew of buccaneers.[214] But Fletcher and most of his crew "refused the pirates" (the pirates "tooke away his carpenter and another man").[215] Angry at losing the prospect of additional manpower, the pirates "used them cruelly" and beat Captain Fletcher "after they had stript him."[216] Fletcher later testified that he believed that "if an Irishmen had not interceeded…they would have kild him with the flat of their curtle-axes [cutlasses]."[217]

The pirates aboard the *Baltimore* plundered almost everything from *Barbados Merchant*, "cut away all his masts, sailes and rigging and bolespritt," throwing them overboard.[218] In addition to attempting to immobilize Fletcher's ship, the pirates "tooke all their candles, broke their compasses, and disabled them soe as they supposed the ship would perish and never give intelligence."[219] Luck was with Fletcher and his men, however, as the mainmast clung to the ship, tangled among sails and rigging. After fitting up a "jury rig," Fletcher and the *Barbados Merchant* made their way toward Virginia.[220]

As *La Paix* approached the ships, Guittar hailed his quartermaster and crew aboard the trailing pink to follow *La Paix* as they continued their way toward Cape Henry, Cape Charles and the entrance to the Chesapeake Bay, "but they took no notice of the signall, and he never saw him again."[221]

La Paix continued on without the pink or the brigantine, on its course toward Virginia. As they neared the capes (Guittar described the distance as eighty to one hundred leagues) around April 22, the sloop *George* came into view. After a brief chase by *La Paix*, *George*'s master Joseph Forrest had its colors struck. After the provisions and other contents of the sloop were removed by the buccaneers and the crew taken aboard *La Paix*, the Pennsylvanian ship *George* was lit on fire while the pirates' carpenter "bored a hole in her side" and burned it so that Forrest and his crew could not warn Virginians of Guittar's approach.[222]

10

"THEIR DESIGNE WAS FOR TAKING ANY SHIPP"

Another day brought another potential prize for *La Paix*. While it was on its way from England to Philadelphia, Samuel Harrison's *Pennsylvania Merchant* settled about seventy miles from Cape Henry, waiting for the wind to pick up enough for it to continue its voyage. Unfortunately for Harrison, when the wind picked up around eight o'clock in the morning, one of *La Paix*'s consorts peeked on the horizon flying Dutch colors as they approached the merchant (likely to avoid suspicion from among the crew of *Pennsylvania Merchant*).

As the pirates positioned themselves with an advantageous wind, Captain Harrison "saw their designe was for taking any shipp then and went to the norward," reacting quickly to steer *Pennsylvania Merchant* into the wind and away from danger.[223] On the run from the pirates, the *Pennsylvania Merchant* approached Fletcher and the *Barbados Merchant*, which was still in the process of rigging its jurymast.[224] Harrison "called to her," and the *Barbados Merchant* "said the pyrates had left her so."[225]

Before Harrison could offer any assistance to the *Barbados Merchant*, *La Paix* again came into sight, goading the *Pennsylvania Merchant* to strike its colors. Harrison refused, "bid them keep off or I would fire," and the *Pennsylvania Merchant* continued its flight from the pirates.[226] Guittar continued his pursuit through the night, catching up with the *Pennsylvania Merchant* the next morning. *La Paix* "began to fire small shott" on the merchant vessel, and Harrison had no choice but to strike his colors.[227] Harrison would later recount, "I did not think the shipp had been so bigg over night."[228] But in the daylight *La Paix* showed itself as a formidable foe.

The crew of *Pennsylvania Merchant* were not treated well. The pirates prodded Captain Harrison, demanding to know "what the reason was I did not strike before." Harrison's response was simple, elegant and seldom accurate, "because there was peace with all the world."[229]

The merchant did not carry much of interest for the pirates, so the pirates robbed all those aboard the ship, stripping them of their clothes (pilot John Hoogling was seen, for example, with Captain Harrison's coat) and belongings over a period of two days. The pirates bragged to Harrison about hanging a Dutch crewman from the yardarm when they resisted. The buccaneers knew that if they let the *Pennsylvania Merchant* go, "there might be notice given here where there was commonly a man of warr." The pirates began clearing the ship, moving all prisoners off the *Pennsylvania Merchant*. One of the "pyrates, having lost his hatt," sent prisoner Samuel Harris back on board "the shipp to fetch him another."[230]

While aboard the *Pennsylvania Merchant*, Harris saw pirate John Hoogling (*La Paix*'s pilot, a New Yorker who sailed with the French and Dutch pirates, also noted in the historical record as "Houghling") "in the great cabbin by a fire stooping downe to the fire with a chip in his hand, which he threw upon it, and there was none by it besides, nor no fire but in the cabbin."[231] Hoogling, one of the last two pirates aboard the merchant ship, was setting the ship ablaze at sea.[232] The other aboard was "Captain Harrison's carpenter," who "was ordered to help," by "cutting a hole in the shipps side."[233] Hoogling returned to *La Paix* on the last boat from the burning, sinking the *Pennsylvania Merchant*.[234]

While *La Paix* was cruising and plundering its way toward the Virginia Capes, Governor Nicholson "put an imbargo upon all the homeward-bound ships" leaving Virginia.[235] At the same time, however, Virginia's defensive network experienced a significant upgrade.

The April 15, 1700 minutes of a meeting of the Council of Virginia in James City show that Captain William Passenger, master of the HMS *Shoreham* (a twenty-eight-gun, fifth-rate ship), laid his instructions from the admiralty before Governor Nicholson to relieve the *Essex Prize* and to "attend on that colony."[236]

Nicholson provided Passenger with nine men and a pilot and authorized the acquisition of a sloop to serve as tender, and Nicholson and the council directed Passenger "as to cruizing, victualling, etc." and sent down the following orders:

> *Forasmuch as the most dangerous time of the year for pirates coming upon this coast is now drawing near…you are to go out and cruise in the*

Bay of Chesapeake and about the capes…for the defense of this colony against pirates. All which that you meet with you are to take, sink, burn or otherwise destroy.[237]

Virginia finally had a proper guardship and tender to surprise "any pyrates boates, which shall be sent on shoar in any private places."[238]

Governor Nicholson did not hesitate in delivering to Captain John Aldred the admiralty's orders for him to return to England with the *Essex Prize.* Aldred was directed to inform the council "what things he wants and in what time he can be ready to sail."[239] Major James Wilson and Captain Samuel Bush were ordered by the Council of Virginia to give Captain Aldred "credit and assistance for the careening and refitting of the *Essex prize* in Elizabeth River."[240] Captain Aldred was ordered to immediately "prefix a day for his sailing, giving notice to the merchant ships accordingly that they may take advantage of his convoy."[241] Nicholson must have been ecstatic at the news of Aldred's departure.

Nicholson was not the only Virginian relieved by the arrival of *Shoreham,* which generally "brought encouragement to Virginians," who were still reeling from the prior years' pirate invasion. With its arrival that April, as the waters along the colonial coast warmed, Virginia knew it was "the most dangerous time for them [pirates] coming upon the coast. Several vessels were convoyed out through the capes, but before the month was out, there was to be livelier action."[242]

Nine days after placing his orders before Governor Nicholson and the Council of Virginia, Captain Passenger reported back to the council that he had not yet located a sloop fit for service as his tender. The council "ordered [Passenger] to make enquiry for another and in the meantime to cruize in the Bay of Chisapeake and about the capes thereof for the defence of the colony against pirates, this being the most dangerous time for them coming upon this coast."[243]

As author and historian Donald Shomette so aptly described it, "Governor Francis Nicholson's winter of discontent began to lapse into the spring of a new century, the miserable prospects of pirate invasions of Virginia's Chesapeake waters loomed larger than ever. Only a miracle, it seemed, might prevent the inevitable."[244]

Shoreham would prove to be that miracle.

11

"A RATHER UNREMARKABLE SUNDAY"

April 28, 1700, began as a rather unremarkable Sunday.[245] Governor Francis Nicholson was at Kicotan (Kecoughtan, or modern-day Hampton, Virginia), spending the "balmy spring day" writing and finishing letters.[246] HMS *Essex Prize* was presently careened and otherwise being prepared for its upcoming voyage to England. The *Essex Prize*'s replacement guardship, HMS *Shoreham*, was anchored nearby as Captain Passenger's men replenished its freshwater storage.[247]

Two ships, the *Friendship* (originally of Belfast) and the *Indian King*, "said to be the most beautiful ship in the Virginia tobacco fleet and one of the largest," were both beginning journeys from Virginia between Cape Henry and Cape Charles.[248] The *Indian King* was heavily laden and London-bound; the *Friendship* was "bound for Liverpool with a cargo of Virginia tobacco."[249]

Guittar and his men had been at sea for months and had been a part of several skirmishes. The freshwater casks were also running low aboard *La Paix*, and the ship required repair as Guittar continued his course toward and into the Chesapeake Bay for the relative safety of Lynnhaven or Hampton Roads.[250]

As *La Paix* approached the Virginia Capes on April 28, the *Friendship* and the *Indian King* were outward-bound and about "three or four leagues from Cape Henry."[251] Guittar and his crew focused their attention on "one of the most beautiful merchantmen," the Gloucester County–built *Indian King*.[252]

The *Indian King*'s captain Edward Whitaker made a critical mistake about *La Paix*, "taking them to be honest men."[253] Thinking little of their approach,

La Paix "came jogging along without colours till they came within shott of us then hoisted up a Dutch ensign."[254] The behavior of Guittar and his men alarmed Whitaker, and Whitaker finally "judged him to be a rogue."[255]

Whitaker's last-minute suspicion was not enough to protect himself, his crew or his ship. Guittar lowered the Dutch flag, hoisted "his bloody ensign" and fired a warning shot toward the *Indian King.*[256] Bloody flags, or otherwise red flags, indicated the pirates intended to give no quarter, meaning they would show no mercy and spare no lives. Edward Whitaker immediately lowered the *Indian King*'s colors, signaling a quick surrender.[257] The classic pirate scare tactic worked, as Guittar and his men captured *Indian King* without any unnecessary violence.

The hands of the *Indian King*'s crew were bound, and the captain and crew were "violently and with force of arms" transferred to *La Paix.*[258] Guittar took the opportunity to interrogate Captain Whitaker, examining Whitaker "about the country [and] whether any men of warr in it."[259] Whitaker "told him that there was none that I knew of, except a small one and I heard she was gone home, not knowing of the *Shoreham.*"[260]

When asked consistently, this type of questioning would have allowed Guittar (and other pirates) to compare information from different prisoners, reexamine other prisoners for more information or take on guides for certain areas. With a full scope of information gathered by thoughtful interrogation, Guitar and his crew could "afterwards lay their schemes to prosecute whatever design they [took] in hand."[261]

Unaware that the HMS *Shoreham*, the powerful fifth-rate man-of-war with thirty-two guns, had arrived to Virginia just days prior, Whitaker confirmed rumors Guittar had already heard: Virginia was guarded only by the HMS *Essex Prize*, the small sixth-rate man-of-war that was, as its captain John Aldred admitted, "undermanned and too small to engage in a fight."[262]

The crew of the *Indian King* was "robbed and terrorized," with their pockets "rifled…amid the terrifying threats and gestures," as the pirates sailed the captured ship into Lynnhaven Bay.[263] Captain Whitaker was examined on what he "had on board, what money, goods or provisions.…Louis of his crew came about me and took what money I had, being about three pounds."[264]

With the *Indian King* captured and under control, *La Paix* focused its attention on the *Friendship*. The intelligence provided to Guittar by Captain Whitaker emboldened the buccaneer, who mistakenly thought he would have free rein over the Chesapeake Bay and its tributaries.

Repeating their earlier successful tactics, the *La Paix* approached the ship and fired warning shots from small arms toward the *Friendship*, killing its captain, Hans Hammel.[265] The loss of the master was too much, and the *Friendship* also struck its colors and surrendered to the pirates.[266] Upon learning that Captain Hammel had been shot, Guittar "seemed to be very sorry and offered to send the chyrugion [surgeon]" but was told by *Friendship* sailor John Calwell that "it was too late, the wound was mortal."[267]

The other pirates aboard *La Paix* showed no remorse about Hammel's death. *La Paix*'s pilot John Hoogling feigned sympathy for Hammel, asking crewmember John Calwell, "Where did your master stand when he was shott?"[268]

Calwell answered, "By the mizen shrouds."[269]

Hoogling then answered, "No, he stood by the mizen mast, and I fired the gun that shott him." And he laughed while Calwell and the *Friendship*'s crew were packed down into the hold with the other prisoners.[270] Four of Guittar's men, including Hoogling, sailed the *Friendship* into Lynnhaven Bay to rendezvous with *La Paix*, the recently taken *Indian King* and the rest of the pirate convoy.[271]

With their prizes secure in Lynnhaven Bay, Guittar once again sailed *La Paix* through the Lynnhaven Roads and into the Chesapeake Bay. Right away, the pirates spotted the *Nicholson* at anchor in the Lynnhaven Bay, about to begin the long voyage back to London. *La Paix* approached the *Nicholson*, showing no colors and pulling within pistol shot. The *Nicholson*'s master Robert Lurtin hailed Guittar.[272]

"From whence you came?" Lurtin asked.

Guittar shouted his reply back to Lurtin, "Out of the sea, you doggs!" And the pirates fired a volley of small arms shot.[273]

Captain Lurtin immediately "slipped my cable, loosed my sailes and made the best of way."[274]

Guittar's men continued to fire at the *Nicholson* and pursued the fleeing ship for almost two hours.[275] Eventually, the pirates shot down the *Nicholson*'s main yard and main topsail and commanded Lurtin aboard *La Paix*.[276] As the *Nicholson* slowed to a halt, Lurtin lowered his flags, and the *Nicholson* was had.

Once aboard, the pirates cleared the hold of the ship, throwing almost one hundred thousand pounds (one hundred hogsheads) of tobacco overboard, along with clothing and materials from the ship, and they took "flower [flour]" aboard *La Paix*.[277] When pressed later about why the pirates threw the tobacco overboard, Guittar gave "no reason for it but saies they men were drunk when they went on board."[278]

Among those pirates who came aboard the *Nicholson* were Cornelieus Franc and Francois Delaunée, who remained on board all night. One crewmember aboard the *Nicholson*, Jacob Moreland, testified that he "had some strong beer and some red wine on board; they [Franc and Delaunée] drunk at their pleasure and so went to sleep."[279]

Although some have described the *Nicholson* as a "clean sloop" that "caught the fancy of the pirates," who intended to keep it, Guittar would later say that "he did not design to make a pyrate shipp of her by reason she was not a good sailor."[280] Guittar watched as his prisoners moved sails and provisions from *Indian King* to the *Nicholson*.[281]

Rewarding themselves for several weeks of hard sailing and their successful taking of several prizes, the pirates continued to drink "strong beer and some red wine…at their pleasure." They "tyed up [the crew of the *Nicholson*] by the hands, beaten with ropes and they struck them upon their backs with their cutlasses," breaking at least one cutlass before some of the pirates fell asleep.[282]

As they did previously with Captain Whitaker, Guittar and his men used the opportunity to interrogate the prisoners about Virginia's defenses. All of the prisoners, except for one (the carpenter aboard the *Nicholson*), indicated there was no guardship in the Chesapeake Bay.[283] Perhaps only the carpenter knew better, but he advised Guittar that there was, in fact, "a man-of-warr [the *Shoreham*] in the country."[284]

To the pirates, the carpenter was obviously trying to trick them into fearing there was a real threat nearby. One of the pirates "took a flint out of the lock of a Gunn and put [it] in his thumb and screwed it in."[285] As interest in that gruesome spectacle waned, the pirates went about beating the carpenter, telling him "he should not lye the next time."[286]

Admiralty Judge Edward Hill later succinctly summarized the pirates' mistake: "Had they taken his word, it would have been better for them."[287]

12

"IN READINESS WITH THEIR ARMS AND AMMUNITION"

While the buccaneer captain and his crew terrorized the mouth of the Lynnhaven River and Chesapeake Bay between the Virginia Capes, Governor Nicholson spent the afternoon in the company of Colonel William Wilson (commander of the militia of Elizabeth City County) and *Shoreham* captain William Passenger.[288] The social visit was interrupted by Captain Aldred (commander of the *Essex Prize*).

Aldred had just been aboard a pink bearing bad news, "Governor Nicholson," Aldred would say, "there are three or four ships or vessels in Lynhaven-bay, who are supposed to be pyrates."[289]

Governor Nicholson took immediate action. It was then between 3:00 and 4:00 p.m. as Governor Nicholson sat down to issue orders to county officers in York (immediately adjacent to Elizabeth City County, where Kicotan was located and which Governor Nicholson's current companion, Colonel William Wilson, was in charge), Gloucester, Middlesex, Lancaster, Northumberland, Westmoreland, Warwick, James City, Norfolk, Princess Anne, Nansemond and Isle of Wight Counties to prepare the militia and alert ships in the nearby rivers.

Through his dispatch, Nicholson commanded militia leaders that "all officers and souldiers under your comand" shall "be in readiness with their armes and amunition at one houres warning as you shall receive further orders."[290]

While Nicholson wrote, Captain Passenger withdrew from his meeting with Nicholson and was rowed back out to the *Shoreham*. The men who

Burning the Ship, an illustration of pirates in a longboat at night, by Howard Pyle. *From Howard Pyle and Merle De Vore Johnson, eds.,* Book of Pirates: Fiction, Fact & Fancy Concerning the Buccaneers & Marooners of the Spanish Main *(New York: Harper and Brothers, 1921), Wikimedia Commons.*

had been filling its water casks were commanded back to the *Shoreham* and requests were made to all nearby ships to send reinforcements; the *Essex Prize* sent eight sailors.[291]

Even with reinforcements, the *Shoreham* was "very weakly manned, several of her men appearing raw and unskilful, and there being many boys amongst them," a far cry from the romanticized description from *The London Post with Intelligence Foreign and Domestick*, which later referred to the *Shoreham* crew as "stout men."[292]

After dispatching his orders, Governor Francis Nicholson, accompanied by Captain Aldred, Peter Heyman and Joseph Manns, joined Captain Passenger aboard the *Shoreham* around 10:00 p.m.[293] Captain Passenger had "got her under saile, designeing to goe downe in the night" to engage the sea rovers.[294] Aldred, of course, was the captain of *Essex Prize*, Heyman was the collector of customs for the lower district of James River and a friend of Nicholson and Manns was a thirty-year-old "able seaman" who had been at Kecoughtan for the meeting between Nicholson, Wilson and Passenger.[295]

Colonel Charles Scarborough, the chief magistrate of the Eastern Shore, a member of the governor's council and the collector of customs in his district, had been laid wind-bound near Reverend Francis Makemie's (considered the founder of Presbyterianism in the United States) home along the Elizabeth River before encountering Captain Passenger aboard the *Shoreham* near Old Point Comfort.[296] Captain Passenger advised Colonel Scarborough and Reverend Makemie that "a pirat had pursued that ship and taken others." Passenger continued, "I desire you would not adventure into the bay but lye at the poynt."[297] Passenger hastily "loosed [the *Shoreham*] and went to turn out of the river."[298]

13

"BROIL *!* BROIL *!* BROIL *!*"

Before sunrise, Captain Passenger, Governor Nicholson and the *Shoreham* were situated on the back of the "horshooe," a sandy shoal that ran from the shore north of Old Point Comfort, eastward toward the channel between Cape Charles and Cape Henry, "standing down towards three ships in Lyn haven bay."[299] With "the wind being contrary and night coming on, [the *Shoreham*] anchored about three leagues short of the pirate."[300]

The *Shoreham*'s approach did not go unnoticed. Captain Whitaker, commander of the *Indian King* under the pirate's control, "saw the man-of-warr that day coming down James River" and saw it again the next morning.[301] Whitaker promptly alerted Captain Guittar that a "great shipp" was approaching and was not far away. Guittar ignored the captain, responding, "'You say there is no man-of-warr here, and if it be a merchantman, I will have him by and by,' and for some time, took no further notice" of the *Shoreham*.[302]

With dawn beginning to slowly break, the *Shoreham* was "within half a mile of the pirate" by 4:00 a.m., while Guittar and the pirates continued to plunder the *Nicholson* and the *Indian King*.[303] The men of the *Shoreham*, however, readied themselves for a fight.

La Paix soon "got under sail, with a design to get to windward and board" the *Shoreham*, pulling close enough for Captain Passenger to hear Guittar shout, "This is but a small fellow; we shall have him presently."[304]

Passenger "guessed his intention and kept to windward," "threw abroad the king's Jack flagg and Ancient [ensign]" and fired one shot at the pirates

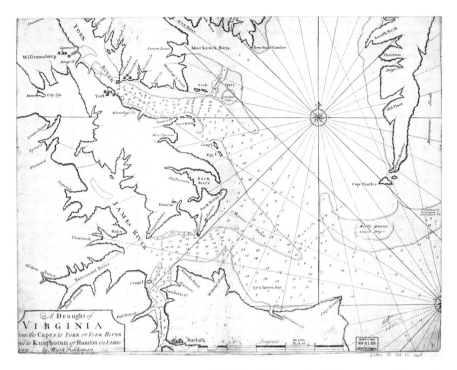

A draught of Virginia from the capes to York in York River and to Kuiquotan or Hamton in James River, circa 1737, with the "Horse Shooe" labelled. *Courtesy of the Library of Congress, Geography and Map Division.*

at "about 7 a clock in the morning."[305] Guittar "immediately hoists a Jack, ensign, with a broad pendent all red," showing his "blood red colloures," returned the *Shoreham* "thanks" and "refused to submit[.]"[306]

With the sun rising at the pirate's back, the true size and scale of Guittar's opponent became obvious. The light shone against half of the *Shoreham*'s guns and lit the decks full of armed men, ready for battle. Guittar, now realizing how formidable of an opponent the *Shoreham* was, called for his men to consolidate about his flagship, *La Paix*.

The crew of *La Paix* cheered, taunting and shouting at their English counterparts.[307] Emboldened by their recent victories, the French buccaneers boasted that they were strong enough to repel any attack.[308] With the pirates' intentions clear that they would not submit and would offer no quarter, the *Shoreham* "immediatly engaged" *La Paix*.[309] Guittar "imediately gott to sail and stood directly with Capt. Passenger," attempting to sail *La Paix* to the *Shoreham*'s windward side before pulling in close enough to board the ship.[310]

Passenger anticipated Guittar's strategy and "got the weather gage," using the wind to his advantage, and what immediately followed was, in spectator Colonel Scarborough's words (who was a full spectator during the entire engagement), "as sharp a dispute as (I thinke) could be betwixt two ships."[311]

Both ships immediately released broadsides within relatively close range and engaged in an "obstinate fight."[312]

As soon as the firing began, the pirates locked the existing prisoners into the hold of *La Paix*.[313] Aboard the *Nicholson*, other prisoners had been forced to work, moving items back and forth from the *Nicholson* to the *Indian King*.[314] The pirates posted aboard the *Nicholson* had found a stock of beer aboard the sloop and were in a drunken stupor when the firing began.[315] The gunshots woke the drunken pirates, angering them. The pirates took their anger out on the prisoners aboard the *Nicholson*, "beating them across the backs with leaded rope ends."[316]

Harbor Scene: An English Ship with Sails Loosened Firing a Gun, circa 1704–49. *From Wikimedia Commons.*

The battle raged into the afternoon, "the major part of which time [the ships remained] within pistol shot of one another."[317] Captain Passenger proved to be a superior tactician and seaman, "sailing something better than the pirate," managing to stay windward of *La Paix*, which was Guittar's "design," despite "a fine top gallant gale of wind."[318] If the pirates got windward, according to their pilot John Hoogling, "then they would 'take the doggs on board them.'"[319]

Customs official Peter Heyman spent the battle on the quarterdeck beside Governor Nicholson, with both men firing pistols across the water at the pirates.[320] Nicholson provoked the men of the *Shoreham* into fevered action as he "encouraged his men with gifts," shouting promises of "plenty of gold" to those that killed the enemy and elevating "their spirits with a cup of good punch."[321]

According to Joseph Manns (immediately to his right), shortly after noon customs official Peter Heyman continued firing "severall shots into the pirates shipp, and [at] about one or two of the clock was by a shott from the pirates shipp, unhappily slaine."[322] Heyman, a trusted friend of Governor Nicholson, had been killed at the governor's side by a shot from *La Paix*. The minutes of a later meeting of the Council of Virginia confirmed that Heyman "behaved very well in the fight" and showed "great courage."[323]

Among the pirates, *La Paix*'s pilot John Hoogling (who previously admitted to killing Captain Hammel of the *Friendship*) appeared to be the true leader and was a "man in great esteem" of *La Paix*'s crew.[324] At one point during the engagement, Hoogling "came into the hold and some askt him how matters went, to which he answered, 'Damn her, she is but a little toad, no bigger that we are. We shall have her presently.'"[325]

The battle was "briskly maintained from soon after sunrise untill about 4 afternoon," with the *Shoreham* taking the advantage by early afternoon.[326] The *Shoreham* shot *La Paix*'s "masts and rigging to shatters, unmounted several guns and [the] hull [was, by that time] almost beaten to pieces."[327] *La Paix* had "disintegrated under the continuous pounding."[328]

Guittar did all that he could to avoid further damage, and "being very near the shore, he put his helm a-lee, so the ship came about, but he having no braces, bowlines nor sheets to haul his sails about," could not escape.[329] Guitar had lost control of *La Paix* as it began "drifting aimlessly [and] shuttered to stop as she ran aground."[330]

The *Shoreham* was unrelenting and maintained its barrage of "small shot and partrige so fast that [it made] all…[Guittar's] men run into the hold, so the ship drove on shore with all her shattered sails aback."[331] Passenger "let go" of the *Shoreham*'s anchor in three fathoms of the Lynnhaven Bay's water, "left off firing" and waited for Guittar to surrender.[332]

The crew of *La Paix* laid a powder train to a collection of thirty barrels of unused gunpowder below deck and "threatened to blow the ship up."[333] It was clear to the prisoners held on *La Paix* that its crew of "resolute fellows would certainly blow up the ship," killing everyone onboard, including the crew and English prisoners.[334] For the pirates, who "went to prayers upon" whether to blow up the ship, "if they could not have quarter, it were as good for them to be blown up and dye altogether in the shipp."[335] Guittar had other plans, however, and "a great many people reported he did design to blow it up, but he did not, for he sett two men to stand continually where the powder was left."[336]

The prisoners begged Guittar to allow them to alert Captain Passenger and Governor Nicholson of their predicament, but he initially refused.[337] The prisoners were relieved, however, when one captive, Baldwin Mathews (captured by the pirates from the *Indian King*), escaped, jumping ship and making a swim for it.[338] Their relief was short-lived as Mathews swam away from the *Shoreham* and toward shore; Mathews was determined to save himself.[339]

The pirate crew taunted the English, chanting "broil, broil, broil."[340] The prisoners below deck knew they were doomed unless Passenger granted quarter to the crew of *La Paix*. One prisoner, John Lumpany (a crewmember and now prisoner from aboard the *Pennsylvania Merchant*), was granted permission by Louis Guittar to swim to the *Shoreham*.[341] Guittar bid Lumpany to "have a good courage" and gave clear instruction: "Tell the commander in chief if he will not give me and my men quarter and pardon, I will blow the shipp up, and we will all dye together."[342]

Lumpany arrived at the *Shoreham*, relaying Captain Guittar's message to Captain Passenger and Governor Nicholson. Nicholson, seeing that "so many prisoners that were His Majesty's subjects, thought fit to send them word under his hand and lesser seal they should be all referred to the king's mercy, with the proviso they would quietly yield themselves up prisoners of war."[343]

Nicholson sat down and wrote out the following response:

> *Virginia SS: On board His Majesty's shipp, the* Shorham, *off Cape Henry this 29th day of April 1700 between 4 and 5 of the clock past meridiem. Whereas, Captain Lewis, commander of the* La Paix, *he offered to surrender himself, men and shipps, together with what effects*

thereto belongeth, provided he may have quarter, which I grant him on performance of the same, and refere him and his men to the mercy of my royall master, King William the 3rd, who God preserve.

Given under my hand and lesser seal at armes the day and year above written.

Fr. Nicholson[344]

Through the "nimbleness of the governour's men" and the mere humanity of Guittar in assigning guards to the powder, an explosion on *La Paix* and killing of the hostages was prevented.[345]

14

"THE PIRATE STRUCK HIS BLOODY COLORS"

Finally, between 4:00 and 5:00 p.m., after ten hours of battle, "the pirate struck his bloody collours and hoisted up a flagg of truce and then fired no more gunns."[346] On behalf of himself and most of his men, Guittar accepted the terms of Nicholson's offer. In all, Nicholson, Passenger and the crew aboard the *Shoreham* used more than 30 barrels of gunpowder and unloaded 1,671 rounds in the direction of *La Paix*.[347]

Three or four pirates, including pilot John Hoogling, leapt into Lynnhaven Bay to escape and avoid surrender.[348]

The attempted escape by Hoogling and others was witnessed from the shore by local resident Nathaniel Mackelanahan, who ran to meet the men. According to Mackelanahan, only Hoogling swam ashore near him.[349]

Mackelanahan quizzed Hoogling. "Can you speak English?"

"Yes," replied Hoogling.

"What countryman are you?"

"I'm of New York."

"Are you one of the pirates?" Mackelanahan asked suspiciously.

"No," said Hoogling, "I was a prisoner forced."[350]

"Why did you come ashore?"

"For a boat."

Shortly after, Hoogling showed Mackelanahan a paper written in Dutch (which Mackelanahan could not read). Other men began to arrive to the shore, and according to Mackelanahan, Hoogling "seemed to be very fear full."[351]

As the *Shoreham*'s boat arrived, Hoogling exclaimed, "Make haste from the shore.…The pyrates designed to blow up their shipp!"[352] This tactic was effective in scattering the onlookers, leaving Hoogling alone again with Mackelanahan. Hoogling used the opportunity to slip away, but Mackelanahan was able to rally the onlookers back to the area and detain Hoogling again. Mackelanahan instructed "a shoemaker to keep him" because "his fingers were swelled, which made me tell him I took him for a rogue and believed he had fought, but he excused himself and said he was forct to hand powder."[353]

With Guittar's surrender, Captain Passenger commanded a boat and small crew to board *La Paix*; 124 pirates were taken prisoner and brought aboard the *Shoreham*, and between 40 and 50 English prisoners "were redeemed, whome the pirate had taken."[354]

Passenger's men reported that between twenty-five and thirty pirates were killed in the battle, with twelve or fourteen wounded.[355] These reports do not likely represent the actual numbers of dead and wounded from among the pirates. As the French pirates were killed and severely wounded during the battle, the pirates threw the bodies of many over the side of the ship (dead or alive).[356] Four men, including Peter Heyman, were killed aboard the *Shoreham* during the firefight.[357]

Upon the request of Captain Passenger, the French prisoners were put on shore in custody of the officers of militia in Elizabeth City County. Passenger was apprehensive of the danger of an uprising if they continued on board.[358] Eight of the wounded men were being tended to at the local home of John Smith but died on the night of May 4.[359]

Following the battle, praise was heaped on Captain Passenger. Colonel Scarborough's account of the battle to Governor Nicholson described Passenger as having "behaved himself with much courage and good conduct, haveing [*sic*] to deal with an enemy under a desperate choice of killing or hanging, and I believe few men in their circumstances but would elect the first."[360]

The three known pirate outlaws (Hoogling, Franc and Delaunée) were not on the run long. Governor Nicholson placed a bounty on each of their heads.[361] John Hoogling made it to the shore of the Lynnhaven Bay but was captured. The other two, Cornelius Franc and François Delaunée, were taken out of one of the recovered merchant ships.[362] These three pirates were not included in the conditions of surrender from Nicholson (promising a trial in England); these three pirates would be tried for their crimes in Virginia.[363]

A commission for their trial at Elizabeth City County Courthouse was ordered by the Council of Virginia.[364] In addition to Justice Edward Hill, fourteen other commissioners were appointed. Five of the appointed commissioners were members of the Council of Virginia, and nine were local residents.[365] Peter Beverley of Gloucester County served as the clerk of court.[366] Cornelius Franc spoke only French, necessitating the use of interpreters (Stephen Fouace, the rector of Bruton Parish Church in Williamsburg, and Isaac Jemart, a merchant and parishioner of Bruton Parish, served as interpreters). A John Vriling served as a Dutch interpreter for one of the witnesses. John Hollier "the shorthand writer," transcribed the entirety of the trial proceedings.[367]

Juries were impaneled by Elizabeth City County sheriff Walter Bayliss on May 13, 1700.[368] The other pirate prisoners, including Captain Louis Guittar, who were still waiting to be sent to England for their own trial, were examined, and their depositions were taken.[369] Virginia's attorney general Bartholomew Fowler set the tone for the trials, arguing that piracy is among

> *the worst of crimes, and pyrates the worst of men, nay by those base actions they degrade themselves' below the rank of men and become beasts of prey and are worse than the worst of enemy's, for they are governed by no laws of nature or of armes they never give quarter, nor show mercy, but as they please themselves live by raping and violence, declare no warr and you are enemy's to all mankind (a good ready why all mankind should be enemy's to them). They violate all the laws of God and man without any remorse or regret. They love mischief for mischief sake and will do what mischief they can, tho it will bring no advantage to themselves. They destroy trade and therefore defraud the king of his customes. The king has a large revenue arising by his customes, and if he suffers in that the whole nation consequently suffers for the king is the head and support of the commonwealth.*[370]

Fowler would continue:

> *Pyracy at sea is the same with robbery at land, but worse in its effects, for the mischief is great and more universall and the benefit less to the taker. A pyrate for the sake of a little rigging will perhapps destroy a shipp of ten thousand pounds value besides the mischiefs much more irreprepable then at land for there we all know where to fly for redress and satisfaction.*[371]

The next day, Tuesday May 14, Judge Edward Hill presented the charges against the pirates to the grand jury:

Gentlemen of the grand jury, the occasion which call this court and you hither is very extraordinary, there being no president [precedent] *before of a pyrate being taken within this, His Majesty's colony and dominion of Virginia, for which at this time we have great reason to praise God being thereby delivered from many miserys, depredations, robberies, and perhaps barbarous murthers which which otherwise this country might have smarted under pyrates being a sort of men whose robberys are generally accompanied with the greatest and most horrid crueltys and tortures to the persons of such whose hard fate it is to fall into their hands and very frequently with the most execrable murder of their captives in cold blood.*

Gentlemen, this commission, by virtue of which this court sitts, gives authority to heare and determine, adjudge and punish all treasons, felonies, pyracys, robberys, murthers and other capital offenses that have been committed upon the high seas or in any river, haven, creek or bay within the jurisdiction of the admiralty of England according to law, and consequently, it is part and duty at this time to inquire of them and more particularly such of the said offences as have been lately perpetrated upon the coast and within the bayes of this colony.

Gentlemen, I cannot suspect that you or any of you would omit or neglect any part of your duty upon this occasion which comes within the verge of your understandings, but because, as I hinted before, matters of this nature have not happened in this part of the king's dominions and you upon that score may be unacquainted, I shall endeavor to give you what light I can and with as much brevity as possible to remove some scruples, which may may arise and thereby enable you the better to perform what is expected of you, therefore, presuming you want no directors what to do for as many pyracys, robberies, or other offences as you find acted by the subjects of your own nation, but that you are thoroughly convinced 'tis your duty to present them and to find such bills of indictment as relate thereunto. You are further to understand that the circumstance of a foreigner guilty of pyracy or robbery upon the high sea and brought hither is no way different from that of a subject of the king of England. Such a one being equally liable to the same process and punishment for hiss offences and, therefore, if any such you find upon your inquiry, or if there be any bills of indictment, proffered against any such. It is your duty to find as the case is without any respect to his being [a] *foreigner. All which when you consider, I dare be confident, your proceedings will be regular and without error, as well as partiality, malice, feare, favour or affection.*[372]

After a slow start, the grand jury returned *billa vera* (meaning literally "the bill is true") for all three pirates, indicting them and signifying that the matter was worthy of further consideration, as follows:

> *An indictment against John Hogling, Marriner, for a pyracy and robbery committed upon the shipp* Pensylvania Merchant;
>
> *And an indictment against Cornelius Frank and Francois Delaunnee for a pyracy and robberty committed upon the shipp* Nicholson, *which were given to the grand jury who, thereupon, withdrew to hear their evidence.*[373]

John Hoogling was tried the same day by the petit jury.[374] At trial, Hoogling and the other pirates relied on similar defenses—that they were all pressed into service by the pirates. All "pleaded not guilty and for tryall have put themselves, upon God and the country, &c."[375]

Hoogling, who joined Guittar shortly after his acquisition of *La Paix*, described his impressment:

> [I was] *forced to go on board the pyrate a first, and hence it was being with some others upon an island several daies without victualls, two of us went a hunting. Two houres, or thereabout, after we were gone, we heard a great gun fired in hopes to get up, we made down to the water side and there saw a vessel under saile. The vessel sailed a long shore, fired one or two small armes and came to an anchor. The boat was hoisted out and some men came on shore. We understood them to be pyrates and then I was willing to stay rather than go with them, but none would tarry with me, so I was forced to go along with my company aboard the pyrate vessell.*[376]

Hoogling further testified that he did not want to join the pirates and participated in the piratical schemes against his will.[377] Hoogling attempted to evoke sympathy from the jury:

> *I would have gone home about my business to my family, but the captain of the pyrate* [Louis Guittar] *would not suffer one. He took his cane and shook me and when I came upon deck, he took his sword and drubbed*

me....He [Guittar] *threatened to put me upon an island, upon a rock, if I would not do as they did. All the Dutch men can swear it. I never came with any free will.*[378]

Hoogling even produced a written note as evidence of his purported innocence.[379] The note, it turns out, was written in Dutch by his compatriot, Cornelius Franc, and was interpreted for the court by Isaac Jemmert:

We, underwritten, do declare that John Houghling is forced against his will to say and remained upon the shipp Lapaix [sic] *and the command of Lewis Guittar.*

We have set our hands do witness it to the and no body should trouble him or should pretend he was there by his owne resolve.

Witness our hands, Cornelius Franc &c[380]

For his participation in the battle with the *Shoreham*, Hoogling testified that he jumped overboard as soon as he heard the pirates intended to ignite the powder barrels.[381]

Although the testimony given by their shipmates was that Hoogling showed fear during the battle, it was only done when the momentum of the conflict began to turn against the pirates in favor of the *Shoreham*. The eyewitness testimony was too strong, and the record became clear that Hoogling was an active participant in plundering prizes and abusing prisoners, including, perhaps, the shooting of Captain Hammel of the *Friendship*.[382] His cowardice in the fight would not be enough to save him.

"MUST I BE HANGED THAT CAN SPEAKE ALL LANGUAGES? "

On Wednesday, May 15, 1700, Cornelius Franc and François Delaunée were tried by the petit jury for the battle in the Lynnhaven. Similar to Hoogling's trial, Franc and Delaunée relied on a defense that they were pressed into service by the pirates and did not want to join the crew. And the testimony was clear that "in the morning when the man-of-warr came up, these two men [Franc and Delaunée]…were on board the shipp *Nicholson* asleep—one in the captain's cabbin, and the other in the chief mate's."[383] Once the fighting started between *La Paix* and the *Shoreham*, the prisoners aboard the *Nicholson* sprang into action against the sleeping pirates and "lockt them up in the cabbins."[384]

Franc testified that he was pressed to serve as the pirate interpreter because of his ability to speak multiple languages, and when he was captured, he shrieked, "Must I be hanged that can speake all languages?"[385]

Delaunée's defense was somewhat comical. In order to avoid hurting the English aboard the *Shoreham*, he said "alwaies when he fired directed his gun to fire up into the aire or downe into the water and, therefore, the rest of the pyrates blamed him for not shooting well."[386]

Delaunée was convincing in his defense and was found not guilty for his actions during the battle; Franc was found guilty. Upon hearing Delaunée's not guilty verdict, both the attorney general and judge were livid. The attorney general chided the jury:

> *Gentlemen of the jury, the evidence, in my opinion, against Francois Delaunnee was very full and positive for what he stood indicted, plainly*

> *proving that he was in armes with the pyrates that took the shipp* Nicholson, *that he went on board her with them, that he plundered with them and that he was one of those that kept the possession of her. He was not indicted for beating any body or being more crule than his comrades, and therefore, you would do well to consider your evidence.*[387]

When the jury responded that they had "done according to our consciences," the attorney general continued:

> *If your consciences go contrary to the evidence, I would not have such a conscience—if you have plaine evidence that this man was on board with the rest that took the ship. Your consciences cannot tell you his intentions were different from his actions.*[388]

Delaunée's freedom and innocence were short-lived, however, and the next day, he was tried and convicted for acts of piracy against the *Pennsylvania Merchant.*[389]

"NOTHING BUT EXTRAORDINARY MEANS CAN REMEDY THIS GREAT EVIL"

E ven though the three pirates were destined to be hanged, their plague of Virginia was not over. While imprisoned and awaiting execution, the pirates escaped the custody of Major John Thorowgood, who was once the sheriff of Princess Anne County.[390]

Governor Nicholson reacted quickly, issuing a £20 bounty on the pirates, sending warrants to every county in Virginia and ordering Major Thorowgood and the sheriffs of Norfolk and Nanjemum (Nansemond, now the city of Suffolk) to forward copies of the warrants to their counterparts in North Carolina.[391] Nicholson would also urge his Carolinian counterpart Henderson Walker to join the search and "give suitable directions for apprehending seamen suspected of piracy."[392]

The pirates headed north and somehow made it across the Chesapeake Bay before being arrested in Accomack County on Virginia's Eastern Shore.[393]

Upon their return to Princess Anne County, John Hoogling, Cornelius Franc and François Delaunée were promptly hanged, executed even before the other condemned pirates had begun their journeys to England for trial.[394] As a warning to any other potential pirates roving the Lynnhaven Bay, the court directed that the pirates be hanged in Princess Anne County, modern-day Virginia Beach, Virginia (not Elizabeth City County, or modern-day Hampton, Virginia, where the trial occurred), on gibbets "of cedar or other lasting wood," using "good strong chaine or rope 'til they rott and face away." François Delaunée was to be hanged at Cape Henry,

A Gibbet on the River Thames, by Thomas Rowlandson, circa 1790. *Wikimedia Commons*.

Cornelius Franc "at the place where the pyates shipp first engaged His Majesty's shipp, the *Shorham*" and John Hoogling "at the place where he was taken."[395]

A pink of seven pirates and nine prisoners had been left in the Atlantic by Guittar with instructions "to cruise in the lattitude of the capes till they came out to them."[396] At that time, five days after Guittar and the rest of the flotilla sailed into the bay, the pirates were apparently struggling to get enough provisions to continue to cruise or to flee Virginia. Even without any "great guns, only small armes and very litle ammunition," the pirates used their "superiority in fighting seamen" to take a small brigantine loaded with cargo on May 1.[397] The seven crew members aboard the brigantine were "put into a boat and turned a drift, they think because they were too many to be kept on board."[398]

A local resident, Adam Hayes, reported to local sheriff John Thorowgood (Thoroughgood) that he watched from his seaside home as the pirates' pink and the captured brigantine were anchored eight to ten miles south of Cape Henry.[399]

Hayes reported to Thorowgood that at about three o'clock in the afternoon on May 2, 1700, he witnessed "a boat goe from on board the Brigantine, to the Pink," and "after that two boats were Passing and repassing from one vessel to the other till near night, at which time the

Adam Thoroughgood House, Norfolk, Princess Anne County, Virginia, circa 1930. *Courtesy of the Library of Congress, Prints and Photographs Division.*

Pink weighed and stood of to sea."[400] The brigantine remained at anchor into the night but was gone by the morning of May 3.[401]

That same day, the seven crewmen of the taken brigantine drifted ashore and provided a report immediately to the sheriff, who, with his brother Adam Thorowgood, prepared and sent a letter to Captain Passenger.[402] From the reports of the crewmen and Adam Hayes, it was clear to Sheriff Thorowgood that these pirates were associated with "the pyrate you [Captain Passenger] took last munday," Louis Guittar.[403]

The Thorowgoods' letter was delivered to Captain Passenger around 6:00 p.m. on May 3, 1700.[404] At the time, Passenger "had not time to write [to Nicholson] wee being just comeing away, and much company with him," including Benjamin Harrison Jr., and instead sent Harrison Jr. to meet with the governor.[405] Before Harrison Jr. left the *Shoreham*, the brigantine seen by Adam Hayes and described in the Thorowgood letter came in from the Atlantic and met with Passenger.

The brigantine captain confirmed the earlier reports (although his account described up to fifty men aboard the pirate ship). Based on this confirmation, Harrison Jr. reported to Governor Nicholson "that 'tis probable they will lye there, to watch for other ships."[406]

Nicholson did not take the news lightly and again took immediate action against the pirates, writing to Captain Passenger from Jamestown at 11:00 p.m. on May 4. Nicholson knew, as Colonel Wilson, the commander of the Elizabeth City County Militia, knew, that the "longer he [the captain of the pirate pink] lyes, the more harme he do and gather more strength."[407]

Nicholson was also concerned about the condition of the *Shoreham* following the recent battle with Guittar and *La Paix*. Nicholson wrote:

James Town, May 4, 1700,
about Eleven a Clock at Night.

Capt. Wm. Passenger

Sir,

Just now, I received a letter from my friend Mr. Benja. Harrison, with an inclosed one to you from the two Mr. Thorowgoods, a copy of which I here send you. If His Maj'tes ship the Shoreham *under your command be at present capable of goeing to sea to look after the pirates in the pink, etc., I would have you doe it as soon as, God willing, wind and weather permitts: but if the* Shoreham *be not in a sailing condicion, then you may, if you think convenient, sent your boat or boats to looke after the said pyrates, in order either to take or burn the said pink. And I do hereby authorize and impower you to stop all ships and vessells from goeing out of the capes, and order them up to Kiquetan.*

If you cannot be here your selfe either on Monday or Tuesday yet, I would have Capt. John Aldred, commander of His Maj'tes ship the Essex Prize, *be here; in the interim remain*

Your most affectionate friend

If you conceive it proper, you may send the Prize, *which you have taken either to take, sinke, or burn the pink on board which are the pyrates. In order thereunto, you may put what men and guns on board you think necessary.*[408]
I hope you have secured for His Maj'tes service the seamen which belong to Capt. Harrison, etc., and you will do the like by those, which Mr. Thorowgood sayes come on shore. And for so doeing these things, this shall be your sufficient warrant and authority given under my hand the day and year above written.

Both the *Essex Prize* and the *Shoreham* put out in search of the pirate pink, but it was never located.[409] The pirates had fled Virginia's waters.

Three days later, on May 7, Governor Nicholson would address Captains Passenger and Aldred directly in front of the council, thanking "them for their service in taking the pirate." In recognition of Captain Passenger's bravery and courage, Nicholson "gave his part of the prize to Capt. Passenger, and directed him to send him his journal."[410]

Nicholson did not forgo an opportunity, however, to advocate for additional resources to secure the waterways that made up the borders of Virginia. Governor Nicholson spoke to the council directly, making it clear that "he had observed that the *Shoreham* was very weakly manned, several of her men appearing raw and unskilful, and there being many boys amongst them."[411]

Although Captain Passenger's answer "that, it being a time of peace, the full complement of men was not allowed as was usual in time of war," the response was not acceptable to Nicholson. In reality, Virginia was, "in a manner, [in] open war, the coasts being daily infested by pirates," buccaneers, sea rovers, smugglers and freebooters.[412] "For certainly," Nicholson would say, "we are in a state of war with the pirates, expecting them upon our coasts, and many be within the capes all this summer. Those great rogues and enemies to all mankind are sensible of their condition if they be taken, which naturally makes them very desperate."[413]

Nicholson "recommended" Passenger "write to the admiralty and desire his full complement" of support as if Virginia was at war.[414]

The Council of Virginia then ordered the commanders in chief of the militias in Elizabeth City, Norfolk, Princess Anne, Accomack and Northampton Counties "to provide look-outs along the coast to give notice and alarm of pirates to them, and by express to His Excellency, and, if possible, to Capt. Passenger."[415] To that end, "Major Thorowgood" (presumably Sheriff John Thorowgood) was "ordered to provide a boat and hands to be ready for communication with Capt. Passenger," and a £10 reward was offered for the apprehension or killing of any pirate.[416]

As May progressed, the legal fallout from the battle with Guittar and *La Paix* continued. On May 11, through the filing of a libel, Captain William Passenger initiated a prize suit for the "condemnation of the…pirats ship called *The Peace*, with all her gunns, ammunition, tackle, furniture, and apparell, to be devided and proportioned according to the rules and orders of the sea, in such cases made and provided, etc."[417]

The suit was initiated at the court of admiralty at Hampton Town before the Honorable Edward Hill. This local court of vice-admiralty was initially stood up in Virginia two years earlier by Governor Andros, in 1698, and Judge Hill was the first judge appointed to the court.[418]

The libel read:

Virga [Virginia] *ss.*[419] *Att the court of admiralty held at Hampton Town on Saturday the 11th day of May in the 12th year of the reign of our sovereign Lord William the Third, of England, Scotland, France and Ireland king, defender of the faith, etc., annoq Domini 1700.*

Before the Hono'ble Edward Hill, Esqr., judge of the sd court, came Capt. William Passenger, commander of His Maj'tes ship the Shoreham, *and exhibited the following libel in these Words*

Virg'a. ss. May the 11th in the 12th year of His Maj'tes reign, annoq domini 1700.

To the Hon'ble Court of Admiralty:

William Passenger, commander of His Majestyes ship the Shoreham, *as well for and in behalfe of His Majesty as for and in behalfe of himself, officers and company on board the said ship, humbly gives this Court to understand and be informed that on the 29th Day of Aprill last past, in His Maj'tyes said ship the* Shoreham, *within the Cape of Virga: he engaged, fought and tooke a company of pirates or sea robbers which were in a ship called* The Peace, *of about two hundred tons burthen, mounted with twenty gunns, which said company of pyrates or sea robbers in the aforesaid ship for severall dayes before their being soe taken did in an open, warlike, hostile, and piraticall manner assault, attack, fight, take, robb, burn, and spoile severall merchant ships belonging to the subjects of our sovereign lord the king (Vizt.).*

A pinke called the Baltimore, *John Loveday master, a sloope called the* George, *Joseph Forest master, a ship called the* Pensylvania Merchant, *Samuell Harrison master, a ship called the* Indyan King, *Edward Whitaker master, a ship called the* Nicholson, *Robert Lurting master, who in a peaceable and lawfull manner were comeing into and goeing out of the aforesaid Cape of Virga. With their severall goods and merchandizes, etc. and also the aforesaid company of pyrates or sea robbers, in the aforesaid ship, at and upon the aforesaid time and place, in a hostile and warlike manner, did fight His Maj'tes said ship the* Shoreham, *but they being overcome and taken as aforesaid the aforesaid William Passenger, in behalfe as aforesaid, prays condemnation of the aforesaid pirats ship called* The Peace, *with all her gunns, ammunition, tackle, furniture, and apparell, to be devided and proportioned according to the rules and orders of the sea, in such cases made and provided, etc.*

W. Passenger.[420]

The continued presence of pirates near the Chesapeake Bay complicated the logistics of getting the more than one hundred pirates to England. After Virginia's attorney general Bartholomew Fowler approved the conditions of the pirates' surrender, the Council of Virginia ordered that "Capt. Lewis [Louis Guittar] and the other pirates be sent to England as soon as possible in the *Essex Prize* and other ships."[421]

In June 1700, 111 prisoners were loaded onto twenty-eight different ships (to sufficiently separate the pirates so that a group could not overtake a crew and commandeer a vessel).[422] Pursuant to the orders of the Council of Virginia, the pirates' hands were to "be in irons at all times and their legs tied at nights."[423]

While provisions were being made for the voyage, the Council of Virginia ordered the *Shoreham* and *Essex Prize* "to go out and cruize in the Bay of Chisapeake as soon as possible to protect ships coming down to take the opportunity of the convoy."[424] If Passenger or Aldred met any merchantmen within the Chesapeake Bay that were planning to leave the Virginia Capes, the captains were ordered to "to cause them to come into James River to take the convoy."[425]

Louis Guittar was kept alone aboard the *George* of Plymouth, and the English convoy was protected by Captain Aldred and the *Essex Prize*.[426] In continued recognition of the weakness of the *Essex Prize* and its captain, the *Shoreham* served as an additional guardship for the flotilla "in hopes to convoy them safe from the coast…to about 50 leagues without the capes, where the greatest danger is…that being reckoned the distance within which the pirates cruize."[427]

Aboard the *Shoreham* was again Governor Nicholson, who was being "hailed as a hero in the London Press."[428] After the battle several weeks prior, Nicholson would not pass up the opportunity to complete the mission, escorting the pirates through the Capes of Virginia from which they came and out into the waters of the Sea of Virginia back toward England.

Nicholson reflected on the past several months and the difficulties that faced Virginia and the colonies in the months ahead. As the *Shoreham* left the relative safety of the Chesapeake Bay and the capes, Governor Nicholson wrote to the Council of Trade and Plantations to be delivered by Captain Aldred:

> *I thank God that by this opportunity of HMS* Essex Prize, *Capt. John Aldred, commander, I send an account of a French pirate ship being taken, who had on board an hundred and odd men, and a list of the pirate-prisoners*

aboard several ships now, God willing, designed for England, as also of eight of them which died on shore and three which were condemned to be hanged, after which they broke prison, but were caught again and executed.

I send an account by Capt. William Passenger, HMS Shoreham, *of taking the pirate, and I am in hopes that my being then on board was noways contrary to my duty, neither my being now on board and intending to go with the fleet 40 or 50 leagues off in hopes to convoy them safe from the coast, that being reckoned the distance within which the pirates cruize.*

I send a list of the fleet which I ordered Capt. Aldred to convoy to England; their sailing instructions; the receipt for the captain of the pirates, and one for a Dutchman and a New England boy, which are sent for England as evidences against the pirate, with the account of such men on board the Essex Prize *etc. which were on board the* Shoreham.

For it is humbly proposed that Capt. Aldred and the seven men may be evidences against the pirates, as also Joseph Man. In the journal of council, your lordships may see what the council and myself did concerning Capt. Aldred convoying the fleet, and what orders we gave about getting provisions for the pirate prisoners, and the instructions given to Capt. Passenger and Lt. Col. Willson, and to the masters for carrying the prisoners to England, with the reasons why they were put on shore out of HMS Shoreham, *etc.*

I hope in God the quarter I gave them is agreeable to His Majesty's commands of Nov. 10, '99. The reasons which induced me to do it are contained in the trial of the pirate ship. I also hope my sending the pirates home for England will be so too. I enclose letters to and from Governor Blakiston concerning HM advice boat Messenger, *Capt. Peter Cood, by which Your Lordships may please to see of what little service that ship will be, and by the journal of council what is done concerning Capt. Cood. But I am in hopes His Majesty will give orders that the* Shoreham *may have her full complement of men, which is most humbly requested, as you may see in the journal of council.*

For certainly we are in a state of war with the pirates, expecting them upon our coasts, and many be within the capes all this summer. Those great rogues and enemies to all mankind are sensible of their condition if they be taken, which naturally makes them very desperate. I send the minutes of council, June 5, 1700, and hope what is done therein will be approved by Your Lordships; but if otherways, which God forbid, I hope it will not be imputed to an error of my will, but understanding.

It is a very great satisfaction to me that you approve of what I did about having pirates and illegal traders tried in the court of admiralty. With humble submission, I think it will be almost impossible to prevent them in these parts of the world, except the courts of vice-admiralty be well established, especially in the charter and propriety governments, and they to be tried there. But I was extreme glad to hear that the L.G. of Providence had taken three or four very notorious pirates, had them tried and executed.

I think there were no courts of vice-admiralty in these parts in which illegal traders were tried, either in H.M. governments or others, before His Majesty was pleased to appoint, pursuant to the acts for preventing fraud, etc. And the admiralty affairs were done in other very improper courts. I am humbly of opinion that it will be prejudicial to His Majesty's interest in all respects, if such courts be not established on the whole English continent here; for the inhabitants, nay, may be the governments, may in some years pretend custom, and then, when they are grown more powerful, it may be very difficult to get their ways altered. Such courts will make them depend more upon old England both in point of government and trade. These parts, being trading colonies, seem to want and require such a court, in order to keep them within their bounds of dependance, and this time of pirates seems to be very favourable for them fully establishing the courts, and at least to have them set up in each province.

The Rt. Hon. William Pen hath three or four times favoured me with his letters, wherein he is pleased to write that he hath begun to reform matters there concerning pirates and illegal traders, and I hope that he will do it effectually. According to his desire, I have assured him that, what in me lies, I will assist him, tho' I will not pretend to give the ingenious etc. Mr. Pen any advice how to manage affairs.

I think myself happy that you approve of my corresponding with Their Excellencies the Earl of Bellomont and Col. Blakiston, which I hope in God I shall continue with them, as also Mr. Penn, for His Majesty's service. But I am apprehensive that His Majesty's service will not allow me meeting them this summer in Pennsylvania, for I am not willing to be far from the mouth of James River this summer, by reason of the pirates.

And our assembly being to meet, God willing, in September and the general court in October, I shall not be able to go to Pennsylvania or New York till the beginning of November, at which time, if they please, God willing, I'll meet them, because I find your Lordships are willing we should be together. And tho' I will not pretend to the parts of any of them, yet I hope we shall endeavour in some measure to answer your expectations.

I enclose copies of letters to and from Joseph Blake, governor of South Carolina, and hope my corresponding with him will not be disapproved by you, for I hope, as I design, it may be of service to His Majesty; and that he hath given you an account of the French their endeavouring to seat themselves upon the River Mesachippi, which I hope in God will be prevented. When the council meets, what you write concerning the new trade with the Western Indians shall be laid before them, in order to give Your Lordships a further account of that affair.

Signed, Fr. Nicholson[429]

With this letter, Nicholson made his recommendations to the Crown for the further suppression of piracy. There was little more for him to do (although he would issue a proclamation prohibiting strange seamen from wandering about Virginia).[430]

Governor Nicholson, again aboard the *Shoreham*, watched as the twenty-eight ships sailed over the horizon for the pirates to meet their fate at the hands of the high court of admiralty.[431]

Having arrived in London, Louis Guittar and twenty-three of his men were tried before the high court of admiralty, found guilty and executed on November 23, 1700.[432] Another forty pirates, making sixty-three in total (among whom were twelve privateer captains of the "late wars"), were tried and hanged at a later date.[433]

La Paix, still sitting in Lynnhaven Bay, was condemned and ordered to be sold, with the proceeds divided "according to the rules and orders of the sea."[434]

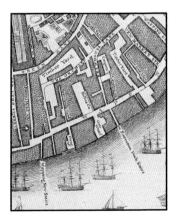

Execution Dock at Wapping, as shown on John Rocque's 1746 map of London. *From Wikimedia Commons.*

After the battle and capture of Guittar and his crew, the colonies were astir about pirates. The reverberations were not, however, caused by the romanticism for "the pirate life" that is reserved for modern times. Instead, the nervous energy existed because these sea rovers, with only a few hands and a solid ship, could terrorize entire coasts and grind trade to a halt. This trade was not simply for economic gain but was required in many instances for sustenance of the colonies.

The Council of Virginia adopted a resolution imploring the lords of admiralty to send or fund additional men and vessels for Captain Passenger, providing:

Upon a serious consideration that our coasts are often and frequently infested with pirates, and in that respect, this country being, as it were, in a continual state of war, the inhabitants being very remote and not without great difficulty to be got upon a sudden alarm, and if continually kept in arms or on board, it will be the utter ruin of their crops and His Majesty's interest thereby much prejudiced; and further considering that Capt. Passenger in his late engagement had not men enough to handle the sails and man the guns, which he hath been several times desired by the council to communicate to the admiralty, but the same is not yet done, this council do hereby humbly submit the same to Their Lordships' consideration, and that the highest complement of men may be allowed to Capt. Passenger, with a small vessel to attend him, that he may be thereby the better enabled to secure these coasts from infesting pirates.[435]

Governor Blake of South Carolina, whose colony was beginning to suffer greatly from piracy, a practice he had (at least tacitly) encouraged began to fall in line, said:

I have seven other pirates that now lie condemned, six of which are at the same time to suffer death, the other, who is the least guilty, I save to be executioner to the rest. I am sure nothing but examples of this nature will put a stop to those barbarous villainies, the sea now so abounding with them that a ship cannot stir for them in this part of the world: the pirate the seven did belong to had in three months' time taken 17 English vessels, and, upon a difference amongst themselves, turned those that we have condemned ashore on our coasts.[436]

The mainland colonies were not alone, however, as pirate sightings were reported all along the route from Bermuda to the Carolinas, with one traveler reporting,:

There are many pirates in the Gulph of Florida; three masters belonging to Bermuda are here, who had their vessels taken by them.... The Spaniards encourage them; the frigates lie in harbour, and all trade will in a little time to these parts of the world be destroyed.[437]

And it was not that the pirate swarms could not be eradicated; it was clear "a few more such expeditious, brave and generous actions from other governments would quickly clear these coasts of pirates."[438] Instead, it was that few men of the time had the courage, means and doggedness to do so—few men other than Governor Nicholson.

In his June 5, 1700 letter to the Council of Trade and Plantations, Colonel Robert Quary (who served as judge of the admiralty for the southern colonies, from Pennsylvania southward and who would later become surveyor general of the customs for Maryland, New Jersey, New York, Pennsylvania and Virginia) confirmed that if not for Nicholson, *La Paix* would not have been taken. In his own words:

> *All the news of America is the swarming of pirates not only on these coasts, but all the West Indies over, which doth ruin trade ten times worse than a war. Nothing but extraordinary means can remedy this great evil, such as H.E. Governor Nicholson hath lately shewn, who did not stay to lose the occasion, but went out immediately in person, and fought a pirate ship of one hundred and forty men, as well fitted and armed as ever men were. The fight continued from eight in the morning till five in the afternoon, in all which time he never stirred off the quarter-deck, but by his example, conduct and plenty of gold, which he gave amongst the men, made them fight bravely, till they had taken the pirates' ship, with a hundred and odd prisoners, the rest being killed. A few more such expeditious, brave and generous actions from other governments would quickly clear these coasts of pirates. I had this account from three men of good credit, that were prisoners on board the pirate all the time of the fight. They assured me that had not His Excellency been in person on board the* Shoreham *galley, the pirate ship had not been taken.*[439]

.

EPILOGUE

Peter Heyman, Nicholson's friend, confidant and official who was killed in the battle, was given a proper burial at Elizabeth City Church with full honors. A copper marker still lies within the neglected and crumbling low-slung brick wall around the foundation of the third church of Elizabeth City Parish (still visible along Pembroke Avenue, near LaSalle Avenue in Hampton, Virginia).

A large, inscribed stone, paid for by Governor Nicholson, remains on the site:

> *This stone was given by His Excellency*
> *Francis Nicholson Esq.*
> *Lieutenant General of Virginia in*
> *Memory of Peter Heyman Esq.*
> *Grandson of Sir Peter Heyman of*
> *Summerfield in the county of*
> *Kent—he was collector of the*
> *customs in the lower district of*
> *James River and went voluntarily*
> *on board the king's ship*
> Shoreham, *in pursuit of a pyrate*
> *who greatly infested this coast after*
> *he had behaved himself 7*
> *hours with undaunted courage,*

was killed with a small shot, the
29 day of April 1700. In the engagement,
he stood next to the
governour upon the quarter deck
and was here honorably interred
by his order.[440]

A smaller, more recent plaque provides:

Peter Heyman,
collector of customs
in lower district of James River.
He went in pursuit of a pyrate
who greatly infested this coast
was killed
Ye 29 Day of April, 1700.

The small cemetery is nondescript and somewhat decrepit, situated now in a fairly industrial part of Hampton, just outside of its downtown and waterfront areas.

William Fletcher, the captain of *Barbados Merchant*, lost his register when he was plundered by Guittar but was granted permission to trade in Virginia with his remaining goods after "making an oath that no foreigner is concerned and giving security that she will unload in England."[441]

Through the summer of 1700, Virginia experienced no disturbance from pirates. Captain Passenger and the *Shoreham* continued to cruise the Chesapeake Bay and capes of Virginia for several months after his battle with Guittar. According to Passenger, the *Shoreham* was in need of repairs and careening, for:

She is at present very fowle, and the ruther is loose, which I fear before the next summer may be of a dangerous consequence by reason he fetches so much away, which cannot be removed without careening or lying ashore, which I presume there is no place in Virginia will admit of.[442]

Following the daring capture of the pirates in 1700, Nicholson would continue his career as a colonial administrator and governor. His continued tenure would not be without controversy, however. In September 1701, Governor Francis Nicholson delivered a speech to the House of Burgesses,

The tombstone of Peter Heyman (Hampton, Virginia). *Author's collection.*

in which he made clear reference to his love for eighteen-year-old Lucy Burwell, the daughter of Major Lewis Burwell. Burwell would decline Nicholson's proposal, but the governor would later write a number of poems to her, which remain available today.

Nicholson would serve as the governor of Nova Scotia from 1712 until 1715 and of South Carolina from 1721 through 1725. Nicholson had been knighted and was, therefore, then Sir Francis Nicholson. Nicholson's attempt to incorporate the South Carolina city of Charles Town (now Charleston) through "An Act for the Good Government of Charles Town" in 1722 failed upon opposition from a group of 120 local Huguenot families.

Upon his voluntary recall to England in 1725, Nicholson, then in poor health, was promoted to lieutenant governor. Poor health and old age did not temper Nicholson's fiery personality and even as late as 1727, twenty-three years after Reverend James Blair published certain charges against Nicholson, Nicholson published a collection of documents refuting those charges.

On March 5, 1728, Lieutenant Colonel Sir Francis Nicholson, former governor of Virginia, Maryland, New York, Nova Scotia and South Carolina, passed away at the age of seventy-two and was buried in the parish of St. George, at Hanover Square in London.

Nicholson's frustrations with his neighboring colonies and leaders "so exasperated Nicholson as to lead him to recommend that they should all be placed under a single viceroy and taxed for the support of a standing army....Francis Nicholson should [therefore] be remembered as one of the very first to conceive and suggest the policy that afterward drove the colonies into their Declaration of Independence."

Nicholson's reputation as a pirate-hunter, or at the least a governor dedicated to securing Virginia's waterways and sea-facing borders, set the tone for other Virginia governors who came after him. Future governors, like Alexander Spotswood, would pick up where Nicholson left off, hunting down one of the most feared pirates of all time, Blackbeard.

NOTES

Chapter 1

1. George Waller, *Samuel Vetch, Colonial Enterpriser* (Chapel Hill: University of North Carolina Press, 1960), 257.
2. "Andros's dispute with 'Dr. Blair in Virginia,' the Earl of Bellomont reported to the Board of Trade in April 1699, 'brought the resentment of the bishop of London and the Church (they say) on his head, which is the reason he has lost his government.'" Kevin R. Hardwick, "Narratives of Villainy and Virtue: Governor Francis Nicholson and the Character of the Good Ruler in Early Virginia," *Journal of Southern History* 72, no. 1 (2006): 39–74, www.jstor.org/stable/27648986.
3. Only three of the six members of the Council of Virginia attended Nicholson's commissioning; Councilmen William Byrd and Richard Johnson were excused because of sickness, and Charles Scarburgh had not received notice of the meeting. "America and West Indies: December 1698, 5–15," in *Calendar of State Papers Colonial, America and West Indies*, vol. 16, *1697–1698*, edited by J.W. Fortescue (London: His Majesty's Stationery Office, 1905), 567–78, British History Online, http://www.british-history.ac.uk/cal-state-papers/colonial/america-west-indies/vol16/pp567-578.
4. After serving as Virginia's governor until 1705, Francis Nicholson would later serve as governor and lieutenant general of Nova Scotia and governor and major general of South Carolina.

5. Mark G. Hanna, *Pirate Nests and the Rise of the British Empire, 1570–1740* (Chapel Hill: University of North Carolina Press, 2015), 216.

6. Reverend Ethan Allen, *Historical Notices of St. Ann's Parish in Ann Arundel County, Maryland Extending from 1649 to 1857, a Period of 208 Years* (Baltimore, MD: J.B. Des Forges, 1857), 32; *see* "America and West Indies: May 1698, 11–14," in *Calendar of State Papers Colonial*, 207–17. "I am heartily disposed to Governor Nicholson. He is really zealous to suppress piracy and illegal trade and was formerly very severe to those who were even suspected of countenancing pirates so that not one of Every's men came to Maryland."

7. Allen, *Historical Notices*, 32.

8. Ibid.

9. Ibid., 32–33.

10. William Stevens Perry, DD, ed., *Historical Collections Relating to the American Colonial Church, Virginia* (Hartford, CT: for the subscribers, 1870), 31–32.

11. Allen, *Historical Notices*, 32.

12. Memorandum of charges against Governor Nicholson, June 23, 1698. "America and West Indies: June 1698, 21–25," in *Calendar of State Papers Colonial*, 278–91.

13. Perry, "Mr. James BLAIR'S affidavit relating to the maladministration of Co. NICHOLSON, Governor of Virginia, 25 APRIL, 1704," in *Historical Collections*, 93–112.

14. Ibid.

15. Ibid.

16. Ibid.

17. Ibid.

18. Ibid.

19. Ibid.

20. Ibid.

21. Ibid.

22. Ibid.

23. Ibid.

24. Hardwick, "Villainy and Virtue."

25. Perry, *Historical Collections*, 125.

26. "America and West Indies: March 1693, 16–31," in *Calendar of State Papers Colonial, America and West Indies*, vol. 14, *1693–1696*, edited by J.W. Fortescue (London: His Majesty's Stationery Office, 1903), 53–70, British History Online, http://www.british-history.ac.uk/cal-state-papers/colonial/america-west-indies/vol14/pp53-70.

27. Ibid.

Chapter 2

28. Hardwick, "Villainy and Virtue."
29. Ibid.
30. Ibid.
31. Stephen Saunders Webb, "The Strange Career of Francis Nicholson," *William and Mary Quarterly* 23, no. 4 (1966): 514–48, www.jstor.org/stable/1919124.
32. This description of Blathwayt as colonial secretary is, admittedly, an understatement. "Translate William Blathwayt's responsibilities into contemporary terms. He was minister of defense; secretary of the cabinet; permanent undersecretary of state in the colonial office; member of Parliament on the government front bench; auditor of imperial accounts; and, subsequently, acting secretary of state for Europe and America and the leading member of the expert, standing commission for the export trade and commonwealth." Stephen Saunders Webb, "William Blathwayt, Imperial Fixer: From Popish Plot to Glorious Revolution," *William and Mary Quarterly* 25, no. 1 (1968): 4–21, www.jstor.org/stable/1920803; Nicholson's service in North Africa first brought Nicholson's name to Blathwayt's attention, and it was Blathwayt who was ultimately responsible for Captain Nicholson's commission that brought him to the American colonies.
33. Offences at Sea Act 1536, 28 Hen 8 c 15 (repealed).
34. Hanna, *Pirate Nests*, 9.
35. Ibid.
36. One of the masters being held by Nicholson described that a pirate prize taken in the West Indies had been taken to Martin's Vineyard (now called Martha's Vineyard), which was traded for "fifty hides and forty tusks," after which, they burned the ship in Port Labarre (Port Royal), Nova Scotia. "America and West Indies: August 1688," *Calendar of State Papers Colonial, America and West Indies*, vol 12, *1685–1688 and Addenda 1653–1687*, edited by J.W. Fortescue (London: Her Majesty's Stationery Office, 1899), 576–93, British History Online, http://www.british-history.ac.uk/cal-state-papers/colonial/america-west-indies/vol12/pp576-593.

NOTES TO PAGES 23–25

Chapter 3

37. Donald Shomette, *Pirates on the Chesapeake: Being a True History of Pirates, Picaroons and Raiders on the Chesapeake Bay, 1610–1807* (Centreville, MD: Tidewater Publishers, 1985), 95–96.
38. "Preface," in *Calendar of State Papers Colonial, America and West Indies*, vol. 15, *1696–1697*, edited by J.W. Fortescue (London: His Majesty's Stationery Office, 1904), vii–xxix, British History Online, http://www.british-history.ac.uk/cal-state-papers/colonial/america-west-indies/vol15/vii-xxix.
39. Ibid.
40. Ibid.
41. "America and West Indies: September 1683, 17–30," in *Calendar of State Papers Colonial, America and West Indies*, vol. 11, *1681–1685*, edited by J.W. Fortescue (London: Her Majesty's Stationery Office, 1898), 495–511, *British History Online*, accessed March 4, 2022, http://www.british-history.ac.uk/cal-state-papers/colonial/america-west-indies/vol11/pp495-511.
42. "Preface," in *Calendar of State Papers Colonial*, vii–xxix.
43. Letter from Governor Nicholson to the Privy Council, June 30, 1697. "America and West Indies: October 1697, 1–15," in *Calendar of State Papers Colonial*, 626–635.
44. Ibid.
45. Hanna, *Pirate Nests*, 216–17.
46. Letter from the Council of Trade and Plantations to governor and Company of Connecticut, February 9, 1697. "America and West Indies: February 1697, 6–10," in *Calendar of State Papers Colonial*, 351–58.
47. Hugh F. Rankin, *The Golden Age of Piracy* (New York: Holt, Rinehart & Winston, 1969), 55.
48. Shomette, *Pirates on the Chesapeake*, 96.
49. Letter from the Council of Trade and Plantations to Governor and Company of Connecticut, February 9, 1697. "America and West Indies: February 1697, 6–10," in *Calendar of State Papers Colonial*, 351–58.
50. See Shomette, *Pirates on the Chesapeake*, 96.
51. Ibid.
52. Nicholson served as lieutenant governor of New York while the province was part of the Dominion of New England (governed by then dominion governor Sir Edmund Andros). When the province rebelled upon the news that King James had been overthrown in the Glorious Revolution, the status of the colony became somewhat in flux. A new governor,

Henry Sloughter, arrived in March 1691; the seated leader Jacob Leisler (for which the rebellion against the prior government was named) was arrested, tried and executed and New York's charter was re-enacted.

53. Letter from Governor Fletcher to Lords of Trade and Plantations, May 30, 1696, "America and West Indies: May 1696," *Calendar of State Papers Colonial*, 1–8.

54. Alice Davis, "The Administration of Benjamin Fletcher in New York," *Quarterly Journal of the New York State Historical Association* 2, no. 4 (October 1921): 213–50, 242.

55. Ibid., 213–50, 243.

56. Letter from Governor Fletcher to Lords of Trade and Plantations, May 30, 1696, "America and West Indies: May 1696," *Calendar of State Papers Colonial*, 1–8.

57. Shomette, *Pirates on the Chesapeake*, 96.

58. Rankin, *Golden Age of Piracy*, 55.

59. Shomette, *Pirates on the Chesapeake*, 96.

60. Ibid.

61. Shomette's description of South Carolina is most interesting, describing the colony as "where wealthy pirates could walk the streets in the open, and the poorest work, unable to pay their way, were frequently hung, their presence was common." Shomette, *Pirates on the Chesapeake*, 96.

62. Letter from Lieutenant Governor Francis Nicholson to Nehemiah Blakiston, September 21, 1690. "America and West Indies: September 1690," *Calendar of State Papers Colonial, America and West Indies*, vol. 13, *1689–1692*, edited J.W. Fortescue (London: Her Majesty's Stationery Office, 1901), 317–25, British History Online, http://www.british-history.ac.uk/cal-state-papers/colonial/america-west-indies/vol13/pp317-325.

63. Ibid.

64. Shomette, *Pirates on the Chesapeake*, 96.

65. Ibid.

66. Letter from Governor Nicholson to James Vernon, June 30, 1697, "America and West Indies: June 1697, 16–30," *Calendar of State Papers Colonial*, 511–28.

67. Rankin, *Golden Age of Piracy*, 54.

68. Ibid.

69. Ibid.

70. "America and West Indies: October 1699, 16–20," in *Calendar of State Papers Colonial, America and West Indies*, vol. 17, *1699 and Addenda 1621–1698*, edited by Cecil Headlam (London: His Majesty's Stationery Office,

1908), 463–82, British History Online, http://www.british-history.ac.uk/cal-state-papers/colonial/america-west-indies/vol17/pp463-482.

71. Rankin, *Golden Age of Piracy*, 54.

72. Hanna, *Pirate Nests*, 246.

73. Ibid.

74. In March 1697, for example, Nicholson petitioned the Council of Trade and Plantations for fifty pounds to be paid to local attorney William Dent, who had been retained by the colony in many customs enforcement matters. Letter from Governor Nicholson to Council of Trade and Plantations, March 13, 1697, "America and West Indies: March 1697, 11–15," *Calendar of State Papers Colonial*, 395–99.

Chapter 4

75. Lloyd Haynes Williams, *Pirates of Colonial Virginia* (Richmond, VA: Dietz Press, 1937), 3.

76. Ibid., 1.

77. Ibid., 2.

78. "America and West Indies: December 1701, 2–5," in *Calendar of State Papers Colonial, America and West Indies*, vol. 19, *1701*, edited by Cecil Headlam (London: His Majesty's Stationery Office, 1910), 630–59, British History Online, http://www.british-history.ac.uk/cal-state-papers/colonial/america-west-indies/vol19/pp630-659.

79. See Williams, *Pirates of Colonial Virginia*, 2.

80. "America and West Indies: December 1701, 2–5," in *Calendar of State Papers Colonial*, 630–59.

81. Davis would later discover Easter Island in 1697.

82. Edmund Berkeley Jr., "Three Philanthropic Pirates," *Virginia Magazine of History and Biography* 74, no. 4 (1966), 433–44, JSTOR, www.jstor.org/stable/4247249, citing "An Accompt of What Plate and Money Was Seized from Edward Davis Lionell Dellawafer & John Hincent," Colonial Papers, F5, 16, Virginia State Library (now the Library of Virginia), Richmond.

83. Perry, "Letter from Commissary Blair to Governor Nicholson, February 27, 1691/2," in *Historical Collections*, 8.

84. Ibid.

85. Ibid.

86. Ibid.

87. Ibid.

88. Shomette, *Pirates on the Chesapeake*, 93.

89. Ibid.

90. Williams, *Pirates of Colonial Virginia*, 23.

91. Ibid., 27–29.

92. Spencer was a London merchant who immigrated to Westmoreland County, Virginia, where he became a planter and which he represented in the Virginia House of Burgesses. Spencer also served as secretary and president of the Council of the Virginia Colony and was named acting governor of Virginia from 1683 to 1684, until the arrival of Governor Lord Howard of Effingham; Letter from Nicholas Spencer to Sir Leoline Jenkins, dated July 31, 1683, "America and West Indies: July 1683," in *Calendar of State Papers Colonial, America and West Indies*, vol. 11, *1681–1685*, edited by J.W. Fortescue (London: Her Majesty's Stationery Office, 1898), 452–62, British History Online, http://www.british-history.ac.uk/cal-state-papers/colonial/america-west-indies/vol11/pp452-462.

93. Letter from Nicholas Spencer to Sir Leoline Jenkins, dated July 31, 1683, "America and West Indies: July 1683," in *Calendar of State Papers Colonial*, 452–62.

94. The *Essex Prize*, a sloop, carried only sixteen cannons (compared to the thirty-two carried by the *Dover Prize*). Shomette, *Pirates on the Chesapeake*, 99.

95. Shomette, *Pirates on the Chesapeake*, 100.

96. "America and West Indies: August 1690," *Calendar of State Papers Colonial*, 301–17.

97. Ibid.

98. Ibid.

99. Ibid.

100. Ibid.

101. Ibid.

102. Ibid.

103. Shomette, *Pirates on the Chesapeake*, 95.

104. "America and West Indies: January 1692," in *Calendar of State Papers Colonial*, 583–96.

105. Shomette, *Pirates on the Chesapeake*, 95.

106. Ibid.

107. Ibid.

108. Ibid.

109. See Hanna, *Pirate Nests*, 190.

110. "America and West Indies: July 1692," in *Calendar of State Papers Colonial*, 663–79.
111. "America and West Indies: June 1695, 1–14," in *Calendar of State Papers Colonial*, 495–513.
112. Henry Every was "a 'pirate king' who was said to have led his fellow crewman from oppression between the decks to a life of unimaginable luxury in a pirate kingdom of their own." See "America and West Indies: May 1698, 11–14," in *Calendar of State Papers Colonial*, 207–17; *See generally* Colin Woodard, *The Republic of Pirates: Being the True and Surprising Story of the Caribbean Pirates and the Man Who Brought Them Down* (New York: HarperCollins, 2008) for an in-depth narrative around Every.

Chapter 5

113. Shomette, *Pirates on the Chesapeake*, 100.
114. "Proclamation of Governor and Council in Regard to Pirates, 1699," *Virginia Magazine of History and Biography* 8, no. 2 (October 1900): 191–92.
115. Ibid.
116. Shomette, *Pirates on the Chesapeake*, 100.
117. *Galley* refers generally to a type of ship that is propelled mainly by oars, with a long, slender hull, shallow draft and low freeboard (clearance between sea and railing). Many galleys at the time also had sails as a secondary means of propulsion.
118. Eric Jay Dolin, *Black Flags, Blue Waters: The Epic History of America's Most Notorious Pirates* (New York: Liveright, 2018), 92.
119. "America and West Indies: November 1699, 21–25," *Calendar of State Papers Colonial*, 536–42.
120. Account by Richard Burgess, master of the *Maryland Merchant* of Bristol, of the attack on HMS *Essex Prize* by a pirate, the *Providence Galley*, in Linhaven Bay and the subsequent boarding of the *Maryland Merchant*, August 13, 1699. "America and West Indies: August 1699, 11–15," *Calendar of State Papers Colonial*, 388–93.
121. Ibid.
122. Shomette, *Pirates on the Chesapeake*, 108.
123. Dolin, *Black Flags, Blue Waters*, 93.
124. Jamie L. Goodall, *Pirates of the Chesapeake Bay: From the Colonial Era to the Oyster Wars* (Charleston, SC: The History Press, 2020), 34; *see also* Dolin, *Black Flags, Blue Waters*.

125. Ibid., 34.

126. Shomette, *Pirates on the Chesapeake*, 104.

127. See Shomette, *Pirates on the Chesapeake*, 104–5, for an account of the storm and specifics about the damage to *Essex Prize*.

128. Shomette, *Pirates on the Chesapeake*, 105.

129. Ibid.

130. Ibid.

131. Ibid., 106.

132. Ibid.

133. Account by Richard Burgess, master of the *Maryland Merchant* of Bristol, of the attack on HMS *Essex Prize* by a pirate, the *Providence Galley*, in Linhaven Bay and the subsequent boarding of the *Maryland Merchant*, August 13, 1699. "America and West Indies: August 1699, 11–15," *Calendar of State Papers Colonial*, 388–93.

134. Ibid.

135. Ibid.

136. Captain William Kidd is, among other things, infamous for burying a small amount of treasure on Gardiners Island off the eastern coast of Long Island, New York. The treasure was recovered after Kidd's arrest and included,

> *Three small bags or more of Jasper Antonio or stone of Goa, several pieces of silk stript with silver and gold cloth of silver, about a bushell of cloves and nutmegs mixed together and strawed up and down, several books of fine white calico, several pieces of fine muslins, several pieces more of floured silk. . . . There was neither gold or silver in the chest. It was fastened with a padlock and nailed and corded about.*

"America and West Indies: August 1699, 28–31," in *Calendar of State Papers Colonial*, 412–20.

137. Account by Richard Burgess, master of the *Maryland Merchant* of Bristol, of the attack on HMS *Essex Prize* by a pirate, the *Providence Galley*, in Linhaven Bay and the subsequent boarding of the *Maryland Merchant*, August 13, 1699. "America and West Indies: August 1699, 11–15," *Calendar of State Papers Colonial*, 388–93.

138. Shomette, *Pirates on the Chesapeake*, 106.

139. Ibid.

140. James would eventually turn his attention to the waters around Maryland. Goodall, *Pirates of the Chesapeake Bay*, 34.

141. Shomette, *Pirates on the Chesapeake*, 111.
142. Ibid.
143. Ibid.
144. Ibid., 110.
145. Rankin, *Golden Age of Piracy*, 67.
146. Shomette, *Pirates on the Chesapeake*, 111.
147. Ibid.
148. Ibid., 113.
149. Dianne Tennant, "Out of the Sea! | Chapter 3: Capture," *Virginian-Pilot*, August 15, 2006.

Chapter 6

150. Letter from Council of Trade and Plantations to the King, January 11, 1700, "America and West Indies: January 1700, 11–20," in *Calendar of State Papers Colonial, America and West Indies*, vol. 18, *1700*, edited by Cecil Headlam (London: His Majesty's Stationery Office, 1910), 25–35, British History Online, http://www.british-history.ac.uk/cal-state-papers/colonial/america-west-indies/vol18/pp25-35.
151. Ibid.
152. The instructions to the Earl of Bellomont were clear; however, these instructions did not apply to Captain Kidd or other pirates for whom the Crown had given specific instruction, "Provided always that our directions herein do not in any wise contradict, alter or interfere with any former orders relating to Kidd or any other pirate signified to you by us"; Letter from Council of Trade and Plantations to the King, January 11, 1700, "America and West Indies: January 1700, 11–20," in *Calendar of State Papers Colonial*, 25–35; *see also* Draft of a Letter for His Majesty's Signature to Ralph Grey, Gov. of Barbados, for Sending to England Such Pirates as are or May be Seized in the Island, February 1, 1700, "America and West Indies: February 1700, 1–5," in *Calendar of State Papers Colonial*, 46–59. (The king ordered Governor Grey of Barbados that he was "to send hither in safe custody all pirates in prison…at the time of your receiving this, and also the witnesses and other evidences which may be of use towards their conviction here. As for pirates that may be seized in…the future, if you judge by the circumstances of any particular case and by the laws in force and disposition of the people that such pirates may be more speedily and effectually brought to punishment there than by sending them hither, you

are to take care that they be tried there, and punished accordingly. But if you judge otherwise, you are to send them hither and in both cases to take care that their goods and effects be secured.")

153. Letter from Council of Trade and Plantations to the King, January 11, 1700, "America and West Indies: January 1700, 11–20," in *Calendar of State Papers Colonial*, 25–35.

154. *See* Letter from Council of Trade and Plantations to Governor the Earl of Bellomont, April 11, 1700, "America and West Indies: April 1700, 11–15," in *Calendar of State Papers Colonial*, 156–70.

Chapter 7

155. *See* Williams, *Pirates of Colonial Virginia*, 21.

156. Dampier was deemed the best authority on the pronunciation and spelling of the word. *See* James Burney, *History of the Buccaneers of America* (London: Payne and Foss, 1816), 43, fn 8.

157. C.H. Haring, *The Buccaneers in the West Indies in the XVII Century* (London: Metheun & Co., Ltd., 1910), 67.

158. Synonymous with *buccaneer* was the term *flibustier*.

159. Haring, *Buccaneers in the West Indies*, 67.

160. "An advertisement to the reader concerning this [first] edition." Quoted in Alexandre O. Exquemelin, *The Buccaneers of America, A True Account of the Most Remarkable Assaults Committed of Late Years upon the Coast of the West Indies by the Buccaneers of Jamaica and Tortuga, Both English and French* (London: George Routledge & Sons Ltd., 1924).

161. See Jeremy Moss, *The Life and Tryals of the Gentleman Pirate, Major Stede Bonnet* (Virginia Beach: Koehler Books, 2019), 9.

162. Yes, even before *A General History of the Robberies and Murders of the Most Notorious Pyrates* (1724), Lord Byron's poem "The Corsair" (1814), *The Pirates of Penzance* (1879) or *Treasure Island* (1883), buccaneers were romanticized in popular literature. Burney, *History of the Buccaneers of America*, n.p.

163. David Head, ed., *The Golden Age of Piracy: The Rise, Fall, and Enduring Popularity of Pirates* (Athens: University of Georgia Press, 2018), 132.

Chapter 8

164. "Louis" is anglicised in contemporaneous accounts, including letters and trial transcripts, as "Lewis," instead of, for example, "Louie"; Harold B. Gill, "The Short and Violent Career of the Chesapeake Pirate Louis Guittar," *Colonial Williamsburg Journal* 22, no. 2 (summer 2000), 36–41; *See also* Records of the High Court of Admiralty, circa 1450–1995, 1/26, British National Archives.

165. Burney, *History of the Buccaneers of America*, 45; Haring, *Buccaneers in the West Indies*, 67.

166. Alexandre Olivier Exquemelin and Basil Ringrose, *The History of the Bucaniers of America* (London: J. Walker, 1810), 90.

167. Ibid., 91.

168. Ibid., 132, 140.

169. Ibid., 193.

170. Ibid., 140.

171. Ibid., 141.

172. Ibid.

173. Ibid.

174. Ibid.

175. Burney, *History of the Buccaneers of America*, 46. ("A certain *Flibustier* captain named Daniel shot one of his crew in the church for behaving irreverently during the performance of mass. Raveneau de Lussan [whose adventures will be frequently mentioned] took the occupation of a buccaneer, because he was in debt and wished, as every honest man should do, to have wherewithal to satisfy his creditors.")

176. Burney, *History of the Buccaneers of America*, 45.

177. Ibid, 46.

178. Haring, *Buccaneers in the West Indies*, n.p.

179. *Barbacoa* is a term still used to describe meat, usually beef, that has been slowly cooked with seasonings. It was popularized in the contemporary mainstream by Chipotle®.

180. Exquemelin and Ringrose, *History of the Bucaniers*, 42.

181. Burney, *History of the Buccaneers of America*, 45; Rankin, *Golden Age of Piracy*, 36.

182. Throughout this book, I use the term *pirate* to describe a general collection of sea robbers, reserving *buccaneer* for its truest sense, using it only when referring to the sailing hunters of Tortuga. With that said, in the late seventeenth and early eighteenth centuries, pirates oftentimes

referred to themselves as *privateers*, a term usually reserved for private ships of war operating under a letter of marque. The Dutch used the phrase *zee roovers*, combining the English words *rover* and *robber*.

183. Gill, "Short and Violent Career," 36.

184. The Examination of the Captain of the Pyrates Taken by His Majesty's Shipp the *Shorham* as it was Taken in a Court of Oyer and Terminer Held at Elizabeth City County Courthouse the 14th Day of May 1700, *The Trials of John Hougling, Cornelius Franc and Francois Delaunee for Piracies and Robberies by them Committed in a Ship Called the* Peace *in Company and with the Assistance of Several Others, Near the Capes of Virginia*, CO 5/1411.

185. Ibid.; see also the testimony of Benoit Pelletier at Records of the High Court of Admiralty, circa 1450–1995, 1/26, British National Archives.

186. The Examination of the Captain of the Pyrates Taken by His Majesty's Shipp the Shorham as it was Taken in a Court of Oyer and Terminer Held at Elizabeth City County Courthouse the 14th Day of May 1700, *The Trials of John Hougling, Cornelius Franc and Francois Delaunee for Piracies and Robberies by them Committed in a Ship Called the* Peace *in Company and with the Assistance of Several Others, Near the Capes of Virginia*, CO 5/1411.

187. Ibid.

Chapter 9

188. The Examination of the Captain of the Pyrates Taken by His Majesty's Shipp the Shorham as it was Taken in a Court of Oyer and Terminer Held at Elizabeth City County Courthouse the 14th Day of May 1700, *The Trials of John Hougling, Cornelius Franc and Francois Delaunee for Piracies and Robberies by them Committed in a Ship Called the* Peace *in Company and with the Assistance of Several Others, Near the Capes of Virginia*, CO 5/1411.

189. Ibid.

190. Ibid.; see also Records of the High Court of Admiralty, circa 1450–1995, 1/26, British National Archives.

191. The Examination of the Captain of the Pyrates Taken by His Majesty's Shipp the Shorham as it was Taken in a Court of Oyer and Terminer Held at Elizabeth City County Courthouse the 14th Day of May 1700, *The Trials of John Hougling, Cornelius Franc and Francois Delaunee for Piracies and Robberies by them Committed in a Ship Called the* Peace *in Company and with the Assistance of Several Others, Near the Capes of Virginia*, CO 5/1411.

192. Ibid.

193. Ibid.

194. Rankin, *Golden Age of Piracy*, 69.

195. Gill, "Short and Violent Career," 36.

196. The Examination of the Captain of the Pyrates Taken by His Majesty's Shipp the Shorham as it was Taken in a Court of Oyer and Terminer Held at Elizabeth City County Courthouse the 14th Day of May 1700, *The Trials of John Hougling, Cornelius Franc and Francois Delaunee for Piracies and Robberies by them Committed in a Ship Called the* Peace *in Company and with the Assistance of Several Others, Near the Capes of Virginia*, CO 5/1411.

197. Ibid.

198. The Examination of the Captain of the Pyrates Taken by His Majesty's Shipp the Shorham as it was Taken in a Court of Oyer and Terminer Held at Elizabeth City County Courthouse the 14th Day of May 1700, *The Trials of John Hougling, Cornelius Franc and Francois Delaunee for Piracies and Robberies by them Committed in a Ship Called the* Peace *in Company and with the Assistance of Several Others, Near the Capes of Virginia*, CO 5/1411; *see also* Records of the High Court of Admiralty, circa 1450–1995, 1/26, British National Archives.

199. The Examination of the Captain of the Pyrates Taken by His Majesty's Shipp the Shorham as it was Taken in a Court of Oyer and Terminer Held at Elizabeth City County Courthouse the 14th Day of May 1700, *The Trials of John Hougling, Cornelius Franc and Francois Delaunee for Piracies and Robberies by them Committed in a Ship Called the* Peace *in Company and with the Assistance of Several Others, Near the Capes of Virginia*, CO 5/1411; "Brandy was especially popular among buccaneers who enjoyed 'all manner of vices and debauchery, particularly to drunkenness, which they practise mostly with brandy: this they drink as liberally as the Spaniards do water.'" Exquemelin and Ringrose, *History of the Bucaniers*, 42.

200. The Examination of the Captain of the Pyrates Taken by His Majesty's Shipp the Shorham as it was Taken in a Court of Oyer and Terminer Held at Elizabeth City County Courthouse the 14th Day of May 1700, *The Trials of John Hougling, Cornelius Franc and Francois Delaunee for Piracies and Robberies by them Committed in a Ship Called the* Peace *in Company and with the Assistance of Several Others, Near the Capes of Virginia*, CO 5/1411.

201. Ibid.

202. Ibid.

203. See Records of the High Court of Admiralty, circa 1450–1995, 1/26, British National Archives.

204. The Examination of the Captain of the Pyrates Taken by His Majesty's Shipp the Shorham as it was Taken in a Court of Oyer and Terminer Held at Elizabeth City County Courthouse the 14th Day of May 1700, *The Trials of John Hougling, Cornelius Franc and Francois Delaunee for Piracies and Robberies by them Committed in a Ship Called the* Peace *in Company and with the Assistance of Several Others, Near the Capes of Virginia*, CO 5/1411.

205. Letter from Governor the Earl of Bellomont to the Council of Trade and Plantations, April 23, 1700 (Boston), "America and West Indies: April 1700, 21–25," in *Calendar of State Papers Colonial*, 190–205.

206. "Deposition of William Fletcher, May 2, 1700," in *Privateering and Piracy in the Colonial Period: Illustrative Documents* (New York: Macmillan, 1923), 262.

207. Testimony of Edmund Ashfold, *The Trials of John Hougling, Cornelius Franc and Francois Delaunee for Piracies and Robberies by them Committed in a Ship Called the* Peace *in Company and with the Assistance of Several Others, Near the Capes of Virginia*, CO 5/1411.

208. Ibid; The Examination of the Captain of the Pyrates Taken by His Majesty's Shipp the Shorham as it was Taken in a Court of Oyer and Terminer Held at Elizabeth City County Courthouse the 14th Day of May 1700, *The Trials of John Hougling, Cornelius Franc and Francois Delaunee for Piracies and Robberies by them Committed in a Ship Called the* Peace *in Company and with the Assistance of Several Others, Near the Capes of Virginia*, CO 5/1411.

209. Testimony of Edmund Ashfold, *The Trials of John Hougling, Cornelius Franc and Francois Delaunee for Piracies and Robberies by them Committed in a Ship Called the* Peace *in Company and with the Assistance of Several Others, Near the Capes of Virginia*, CO 5/1411.

210. Gill, "Short and Violent Career," 37; Rankin, *Golden Age of Piracy*, 69 (includes Lovejoy's name as master).

211. "Deposition of William Fletcher, May 2, 1700," in *Privateering and Piracy*, 262.

212. Rankin, *Golden Age of Piracy*, 69–70.

213. "Deposition of William Fletcher, May 2, 1700," in *Privateering and Piracy*, 262–63; In many instances, a group of pirates would draw up their own code or articles in democratic fashion, which provided rules for discipline, division of stolen goods and compensation for injured pirates. Potential crew members would be asked to sign or make his (or her) mark on the articles, then swear an oath of allegiance or honor. The oath was sometimes taken on a Bible but could be done on anything—there are

recorded instances of a crew swearing on an axe, crossed pistols, swords or on a human skull or astride a cannon. Nine complete or nearly complete sets of piratical articles have survived, chiefly from Charles Johnson's *A General History of the Pyrates*, first published in 1724, and from records kept by admiralty court proceedings at the trials of pirates. A partial code from Henry Morgan is preserved in Alexandre Exquemelin's 1678 book *The Buccaneers of America*.

214. "Deposition of William Fletcher, May 2, 1700," in *Privateering and Piracy*, 262–63.

215. Ibid.

216. Ibid.

217. Ibid., 263–64.

218. Ibid.; see also Letter from the Earl of Bellomont to the Council of Trade and Plantations, April 23, 1700 (Boston), "America and West Indies: April 1700, 21–25," in *Calendar of State Papers Colonial*, 190–205.

219. "Deposition of William Fletcher, May 2, 1700," in *Privateering and Piracy*, 263–64.

220. Rankin, *Golden Age of Piracy*, 70.

221. Gill, "Short and Violent Career," 37.

222. Ibid., 37; Rankin, *Golden Age of Piracy*, 69.

Chapter 10

223. Testimony of Samuel Harrison, *The Trials of John Hougling, Cornelius Franc and Francois Delaunee for Piracies and Robberies by them Committed in a Ship Called the* Peace *in Company and with the Assistance of Several Others, Near the Capes of Virginia*, CO 5/1411.

224. Rankin, *Golden Age of Piracy*, 70.

225. Testimony of Samuel Harrison, *The Trials of John Hougling, Cornelius Franc and Francois Delaunee for Piracies and Robberies by them Committed in a Ship Called the* Peace *in Company and with the Assistance of Several Others, Near the Capes of Virginia*, CO 5/1411.

226. Ibid.

227. Ibid.

228. Ibid.

229. Ibid.

230. Ibid.

231. Ibid.

232. Captain Guittar would later testify that the burning of *Pennsylvania Merchant* "was the pylotts doing, he [Guittar] being no arsonist, himself." The Examination of the Captain of the Pyrates Taken by His Majesty's Shipp the Shorham as it was Taken in a Court of Oyer and Terminer Held at Elizabeth City County Courthouse the 14th Day of May 1700, *The Trials of John Hougling, Cornelius Franc and Francois Delaunee for Piracies and Robberies by them Committed in a Ship Called the* Peace *in Company and with the Assistance of Several Others, Near the Capes of Virginia*, CO 5/1411.

233. Testimony of Samuel Harrison, *The Trials of John Hougling, Cornelius Franc and Francois Delaunee for Piracies and Robberies by them Committed in a Ship Called the* Peace *in Company and with the Assistance of Several Others, Near the Capes of Virginia*, CO 5/1411.

234. Ibid.

235. *London Post with Intelligence Foreign and Domestick*, June 19–21, 1700.

236. Minutes of Council of Virginia, April 15, 1700, "America and West Indies: April 1700, 11–15," in *Calendar of State Papers Colonial*, 156–70; see also Letter from J. Burchett to W. Popple, March 29, 1700, "America and West Indies: March 1700, 21–29," in *Calendar of State Papers Colonial*, 130–44.

237. Tennant, "Out of the Sea!"

238. Minutes of Council of Virginia, April 15, 1700, "America and West Indies: April 1700, 11–15," in *Calendar of State Papers Colonial*, 156–70; Shomette, *Pirates on the Chesapeake*, 132.

239. Minutes of Council of Virginia, April 15, 1700, "America and West Indies: April 1700, 11–15," in *Calendar of State Papers Colonial*, 156–70.

240. Minutes of Council of Virginia, April 15, 1700, "America and West Indies: April 1700, 16–20," in *Calendar of State Papers Colonial*, 170–90.

241. Ibid.

242. Rankin, *Golden Age of Piracy*, 68.

243. Minutes of Council of Virginia, April 24, 1700, "America and West Indies: April 1700, 21–25," in *Calendar of State Papers Colonial*, 190–205.

244. Shomette, *Pirates on the Chesapeake*, 122.

Chapter 11

245. It is important to note that at the time, two different calendars existed—the English-speaking world used the Julian calendar; the French and Spanish-speaking world used the Gregorian (still used today). The eleven-

day difference in calendars has proven to be significant, especially when piecing together English and French sources.

246. Rankin, *Golden Age of Piracy*, 68.

247. Ibid.; Gill, "Short and Violent Career," 38.

248. Gill, "Short and Violent Career," 36–41.

249. Rankin, *Golden Age of Piracy*, 71.

250. Ibid., 70.

251. "Deposition of William Woolgar and Others, June 11, 1700," in *Privateering and Piracy*, 272.

252. Rankin, *Golden Age of Piracy*, 70–71; Gill, "Short and Violent Career," 37.

253. Testimony of Edward Whitaker, *The Trials of John Hougling, Cornelius Franc and Francois Delaunee for Piracies and Robberies by them Committed in a Ship Called the* Peace *in Company and with the Assistance of Several Others, Near the Capes of Virginia*, CO 5/1411.

254. Ibid.

255. Ibid.

256. Ibid.

257. Rankin, *Golden Age of Piracy*, 70–71.

258. Ibid., 71; Gill, "Short and Violent Career," 37.

259. Testimony of Edward Whitaker, *The Trials of John Hougling, Cornelius Franc and Francois Delaunee for Piracies and Robberies by them Committed in a Ship Called the* Peace *in Company and with the Assistance of Several Others, Near the Capes of Virginia*, CO 5/1411.

260. Ibid.

261. William Dampier, *A New Voyage Round the World* (London: James Knapton, 1699), 28.

262. Gill, "Short and Violent Career," 37.

263. Ibid., 37; Rankin, *Golden Age of Piracy*, 71; In 1700, Thomas Lacy and William Woolgar would be provided an allowance of twenty-three shillings per months for five months for their voluntary service aboard the HMS *Shoreham*. "Deposition of William Woolgar and Others, June 11, 1700," in *Privateering and Piracy*, 273; Rankin, *Golden Age of Piracy*, 71.

264. Testimony of Edward Whitaker, *The Trials of John Hougling, Cornelius Franc and Francois Delaunee for Piracies and Robberies by them Committed in a Ship Called the* Peace *in Company and with the Assistance of Several Others, Near the Capes of Virginia*, CO 5/1411.

265. Rankin, *Golden Age of Piracy*, 71.

266. Gill, "Short and Violent Career," 37.

267. Testimony of John Calwell, *The Trials of John Hougling, Cornelius Franc and Francois Delaunee for Piracies and Robberies by them Committed in a Ship Called the* Peace *in Company and with the Assistance of Several Others, Near the Capes of Virginia*, CO 5/1411.

268. Ibid.

269. Ibid.

270. Ibid.; Captain Guittar would later testify that it was the pilot of *La Paix*, John Hoogling, who shot Hans Hammel, clarifying that "the rest of the crew told him so, he did not see him do it." The Examination of the Captain of the Pyrates Taken by His Majesty's Shipp the Shorham as it was Taken in a Court of Oyer and Terminer Held at Elizabeth City County Courthouse the 14th Day of May 1700, *The Trials of John Hougling, Cornelius Franc and Francois Delaunee for Piracies and Robberies by them Committed in a Ship Called the* Peace *in Company and with the Assistance of Several Others, Near the Capes of Virginia*, CO 5/1411.

271. Rankin, *Golden Age of Piracy*, 71.

272. Testimony of Robert Lurtin, *The Trials of John Hougling, Cornelius Franc and Francois Delaunee for Piracies and Robberies by them Committed in a Ship Called the* Peace *in Company and with the Assistance of Several Others, Near the Capes of Virginia*, CO 5/1411.

273. Ibid.

274. Ibid.

275. Ibid.

276. Ibid.

277. The Examination of the Captain of the Pyrates Taken by His Majesty's Shipp the Shorham as it was Taken in a Court of Oyer and Terminer Held at Elizabeth City County Courthouse the 14th Day of May 1700, *The Trials of John Hougling, Cornelius Franc and Francois Delaunee for Piracies and Robberies by them Committed in a Ship Called the* Peace *in Company and with the Assistance of Several Others, Near the Capes of Virginia*, CO 5/1411; *see also* Gill, "Short and Violent Career," 37.

278. The Examination of the Captain of the Pyrates Taken by His Majesty's Shipp the Shorham as it was Taken in a Court of Oyer and Terminer Held at Elizabeth City County Courthouse the 14th Day of May 1700, *The Trials of John Hougling, Cornelius Franc and Francois Delaunee for Piracies and Robberies by them Committed in a Ship Called the* Peace *in Company and with the Assistance of Several Others, Near the Capes of Virginia*, CO 5/1411.

279. Testimony of Jacob Moreland, *The Trials of John Hougling, Cornelius Franc and Francois Delaunee for Piracies and Robberies by them Committed in a Ship Called*

the Peace *in Company and with the Assistance of Several Others, Near the Capes of Virginia*, CO 5/1411.

280. Rankin, *Golden Age of Piracy*, 71; The Examination of the Captain of the Pyrates Taken by His Majesty's Shipp the Shorham as it was Taken in a Court of Oyer and Terminer Held at Elizabeth City County Courthouse the 14ᵗʰ Day of May 1700, *The Trials of John Hougling, Cornelius Franc and Francois Delaunee for Piracies and Robberies by them Committed in a Ship Called the* Peace *in Company and with the Assistance of Several Others, Near the Capes of Virginia*, CO 5/1411.

281. Rankin, *Golden Age of Piracy*, 71.

282. Testimony of Jacob Moreland, *The Trials of John Hougling, Cornelius Franc and Francois Delaunee for Piracies and Robberies by them Committed in a Ship Called the* Peace *in Company and with the Assistance of Several Others, Near the Capes of Virginia*, CO 5/1411.

283. Rankin, *Golden Age of Piracy*, 71–72.

284. Testimony of Jacob Moreland, *The Trials of John Hougling, Cornelius Franc and Francois Delaunee for Piracies and Robberies by them Committed in a Ship Called the* Peace *in Company and with the Assistance of Several Others, Near the Capes of Virginia*, CO 5/1411.

285. Ibid.

286. Ibid.

287. *The Trials of John Hougling, Cornelius Franc and Francois Delaunee for Piracies and Robberies by them Committed in a Ship Called the* Peace *in Company and with the Assistance of Several Others, Near the Capes of Virginia*, CO 5/1411.

Chapter 12

288. Rankin, *Golden Age of Piracy*, 68. See also Records of the High Court of Admiralty, circa 1450–1995, 1/26, British National Archives.

289. Rankin, *Golden Age of Piracy*, 68; "Orders of Governor Nicholson to County Officers, April 28, 1700," in *Privateering and Piracy*, 260.

290. "Orders of Governor Nicholson to County Officers, April 28, 1700," in *Privateering and Piracy*, 262.

291. Rankin, *Golden Age of Piracy*, 68.

292. Minutes of Council of Virginia, May 7, 1700, "America and West Indies: May 1700, 6–10," in *Calendar of State Papers Colonial*, 229–47; *London Post with Intelligence Foreign and Domestick*, June 10–12, 1700.

293. Captain Passenger's Account of the Taking of a French Pirate, June 10, 1700, "America and West Indies: June 1700, 6-10," in *Calendar of State Papers Colonial*, 302–29.

294. "Deposition of Joseph Man, June 11, 1700," in *Privateering and Piracy*, 274.

295. Ibid., 273–74.

296. "Charles Scarburgh to Governor Nicholson, May 3, 1700," in *Privateering and Piracy*, 265.

297. Ibid., 265–66.

298. Ibid., 265.

Chapter 13

299. "Charles Scarburgh to Governor Nicholson, May 3, 1700," in *Privateering and Piracy*, 265–66.

300. Captain Passenger's Account of the Taking of a French Pirate, June 10, 1700, "America and West Indies: June 1700, 6–10," in *Calendar of State Papers Colonial*, 302–29.

301. Testimony of Edward Whitaker, *The Trials of John Hougling, Cornelius Franc and Francois Delaunee for Piracies and Robberies by them Committed in a Ship Called the* Peace *in Company and with the Assistance of Several Others, Near the Capes of Virginia*, CO 5/1411.

302. Ibid.

303. Captain Passenger's Account of the Taking of a French Pirate, June 10, 1700, "America and West Indies: June 1700, 6–10," in *Calendar of State Papers Colonial*, 302–29; Another contemporary account described that Captain Passenger and the *Shoreham* "came up with the pirate" at "about six of the clock." "Deposition of Joseph Man, June 11, 1700," in *Privateering and Piracy*, 274; Rankin, *Golden Age of Piracy*, 72; Gill, "Short and Violent Career," 38.

304. Captain Passenger's Account of the Taking of a French Pirate, June 10, 1700, "America and West Indies: June 1700, 6–10," in *Calendar of State Papers Colonial*, 302–29.

305. Ibid.; "Deposition of Joseph Man, June 11, 1700," in *Privateering and Piracy*, 274; "Deposition of William Woolgar and Others, June 11, 1700," in *Privateering and Piracy*, 273.

306. Captain Passenger's Account of the Taking of a French Pirate, June 10, 1700, "America and West Indies: June 1700, 6–10," in *Calendar of*

State Papers Colonial, 302–29; "Deposition of Joseph Man, June 11, 1700," in *Privateering and Piracy*, 274; Captain Passenger's Account of the Taking of a French Pirate, June 10, 1700, "America and West Indies: June 1700, 6–10," in *Calendar of State Papers Colonial*, 302–29; "Deposition of Joseph Man, June 11, 1700," in *Privateering and Piracy*, 274.

307. Rankin, *Golden Age of Piracy*, 72.

308. Ibid.

309. "Deposition of Joseph Man, June 11, 1700," in *Privateering and Piracy*, 274.

310. "Charles Scarburgh to Governor Nicholson, May 3, 1700," in *Privateering and Piracy*, 265; Rankin, *Golden Age of Piracy*, 72; Gill, "Short and Violent Career," 38.

311. "Charles Scarburgh to Governor Nicholson, May 3, 1700," in *Privateering and Piracy*, 265.

312. Rankin, *Golden Age of Piracy*, 72; *London Post with Intelligence Foreign and Domestick*, July 24–26, 1700.

313. Rankin, *Golden Age of Piracy*, 72.

314. Ibid.

315. Ibid.

316. Ibid.

317. Captain Passenger's Account of the Taking of a French Pirate, June 10, 1700, "America and West Indies: June 1700, 6–10," in *Calendar of State Papers Colonial*, 302–29.

318. Ibid.

319. Testimony of Baldwin Mathews, *The Trials of John Hougling, Cornelius Franc and Francois Delaunee for Piracies and Robberies by them Committed in a Ship Called the* Peace *in Company and with the Assistance of Several Others, Near the Capes of Virginia*, CO 5/1411.

320. Rankin, *Golden Age of Piracy*, 72.

321. *London Post with Intelligence Foreign and Domestick*, June 10–12, 1700; Rankin, *Golden Age of Piracy*, 72; *London Post with Intelligence Foreign and Domestick*, June 10–12, 1700.

322. Rankin, *Golden Age of Piracy*, 72; "Deposition of Joseph Man, June 11, 1700," in *Privateering and Piracy*, 274.

323. Minutes of Council of Virginia, May 6, 1700, "America and West Indies: May 1700, 6–10," in *Calendar of State Papers Colonial*, 229–47; Rankin, *Golden Age of Piracy*, 72.

324. Ibid.

325. Testimony of Edward Whitaker, *The Trials of John Hougling, Cornelius Franc and Francois Delaunee for Piracies and Robberies by them Committed in a Ship*

Called the Peace *in Company and with the Assistance of Several Others, Near the Capes of Virginia*, CO 5/1411.

326. "Charles Scarburgh to Governor Nicholson, May 3, 1700," in *Privateering and Piracy*, 265; *see also* "Deposition of William Woolgar and Others, June 11, 1700," in *Privateering and Piracy*, 273 (Two men aboard the *Shoreham*, William Woolgar and Peter Shaw, swore before the Court of Oyer and Terminer for the trial of pirates that Passenger and the *Shoreham* "forced them [Guittar and the pirates] to surrender about 4 or 5 a clock in the afternoon.")

327. Captain Passenger's Account of the Taking of a French Pirate, June 10, 1700, "America and West Indies: June 1700, 6–10," in *Calendar of State Papers Colonial*, 302–29.

328. Rankin, *Golden Age of Piracy*, 72–73.

329. Captain Passenger's Account of the Taking of a French Pirate, June 10, 1700, "America and West Indies: June 1700, 6–10," in *Calendar of State Papers Colonial*, 302–29.

330. Rankin, *Golden Age of Piracy*, 72–73.

331. Captain Passenger's Account of the Taking of a French Pirate, June 10, 1700, "America and West Indies: June 1700, 6–10," in *Calendar of State Papers Colonial*, 302–29.

332. Originally the span of a man's outstretched arms, the length of a fathom has varied over time. Although it is now accepted that a fathom is equal to 2.000 imperial yards (6 feet), it was previously defined as .001 imperial or admiralty nautical mile (6,080.000 feet, resulting in a measurement of 6.080 feet) and may have, at one time, been closer to 5.000 or 5.500 feet, rather than 6.000; Captain Passenger's Account of the Taking of a French Pirate, June 10, 1700, "America and West Indies: June 1700, 6–10," in *Calendar of State Papers Colonial*, 302–29; Rankin, *Golden Age of Piracy*, 73.

333. Captain Passenger's Account of the Taking of a French Pirate, June 10, 1700, "America and West Indies: June 1700, 6–10," in *Calendar of State Papers Colonial*, 302–29.

334. Ibid.

335. Testimony of Edmund Ashfold, *The Trials of John Hougling, Cornelius Franc and Francois Delaunee for Piracies and Robberies by them Committed in a Ship Called the* Peace *in Company and with the Assistance of Several Others, Near the Capes of Virginia*, CO 5/1411; The Examination of the Captain of the Pyrates Taken by His Majesty's Shipp the Shorham as it was Taken in a Court of Oyer and Terminer Held at Elizabeth City County Courthouse

the 14th Day of May 1700, *The Trials of John Hougling, Cornelius Franc and Francois Delaunee for Piracies and Robberies by them Committed in a Ship Called the* Peace *in Company and with the Assistance of Several Others, Near the Capes of Virginia*, CO 5/1411.

336. The Examination of the Captain of the Pyrates Taken by His Majesty's Shipp the Shorham as it was Taken in a Court of Oyer and Terminer Held at Elizabeth City County Courthouse the 14th Day of May 1700, *The Trials of John Hougling, Cornelius Franc and Francois Delaunee for Piracies and Robberies by them Committed in a Ship Called the* Peace *in Company and with the Assistance of Several Others, Near the Capes of Virginia*, CO 5/1411.

337. Rankin, *Golden Age of Piracy*, 73.

338. Testimony of Baldwin Mathews, *The Trials of John Hougling, Cornelius Franc and Francois Delaunee for Piracies and Robberies by them Committed in a Ship Called the* Peace *in Company and with the Assistance of Several Others, Near the Capes of Virginia*, CO 5/1411.

339. Rankin, *Golden Age of Piracy*, 73.

340. Testimony of Robert Lurtin, *The Trials of John Hougling, Cornelius Franc and Francois Delaunee for Piracies and Robberies by them Committed in a Ship Called the* Peace *in Company and with the Assistance of Several Others, Near the Capes of Virginia*, CO 5/1411.

341. Rankin, *Golden Age of Piracy*, 73.

342. Testimony of John Lumpany, *The Trials of John Hougling, Cornelius Franc and Francois Delaunee for Piracies and Robberies by them Committed in a Ship Called the* Peace *in Company and with the Assistance of Several Others, Near the Capes of Virginia*, CO 5/1411.

343. Captain Passenger's Account of the Taking of a French Pirate, June 10, 1700, "America and West Indies: June 1700, 6–10," in *Calendar of State Papers Colonial*, 302–29.

344. The Examination of the Captain of the Pyrates Taken by His Majesty's Shipp the Shorham as it was Taken in a Court of Oyer and Terminer Held at Elizabeth City County Courthouse the 14th Day of May 1700, *The Trials of John Hougling, Cornelius Franc and Francois Delaunee for Piracies and Robberies by them Committed in a Ship Called the* Peace *in Company and with the Assistance of Several Others, Near the Capes of Virginia*, CO 5/1411.

345. *London Post with Intelligence Foreign and Domestick*, June 10–12, 1700.

Chapter 14

346. "Deposition of Joseph Man, June 11, 1700," in *Privateering and Piracy*, 274.

347. Mark St. John Erickson, "A Daring Governor Shows His Mettle in a Bloody April 29, 1700 Pirate Battle," *Daily Press*, August 25, 2019, https://www.dailypress.com/history/dp-a-daring-governor-shows-his-mettle-in-a-bloody-april-29-1700-pirate-battle-20140428-post.html.

348. Lurtin testified that Hoogling "did swim ashore before" Guittar surrendered. Testimony of Robert Lurtin, *The Trials of John Hougling, Cornelius Franc and Francois Delaunee for Piracies and Robberies by them Committed in a Ship Called the* Peace *in Company and with the Assistance of Several Others, Near the Capes of Virginia*, CO 5/1411; Gill, "Short and Violent Career," 39.

349. If three pirates leapt overboard, as Mackelanahan testified, then two or three other pirates escaped from *La Paix* that day.

350. *See* Testimony of Nathaniel Mackelanahan, *The Trials of John Hougling, Cornelius Franc and Francois Delaunee for Piracies and Robberies by them Committed in a Ship Called the* Peace *in Company and with the Assistance of Several Others, Near the Capes of Virginia*, CO 5/1411.

351. Ibid.

352. Ibid.

353. Ibid.

354. Others would testify to this number of prisoners as well, including Edmund Ashfold. "Deposition of Joseph Man, June 11, 1700," in *Privateering and Piracy*, 274.

355. Ibid.; Rankin, *Golden Age of Piracy*, 73–74.

356. Rankin, *Golden Age of Piracy*, 74.

357. Besides Heyman, Passenger admitted, "The other three, not expecting to be called as an evidence, I have not their names about me and do not remember them." Testimony of Captain William Passenger, *The Trials of John Hougling, Cornelius Franc and Francois Delaunee for Piracies and Robberies by them Committed in a Ship Called the* Peace *in Company and with the Assistance of Several Others, Near the Capes of Virginia*, CO 5/1411.

358. Minutes of Council of Virginia, May 7, 1700, "America and West Indies: May 1700, 6–10," *Calendar of State Papers Colonial*, 229–47.

359. "William Wilson to Governor Nicholson, May 5, 1700," in *Privateering and Piracy*, 269–70; see also Governor Nicholson to the Council of Trade and Plantations, June 10, 1700, "America and West Indies: June 1700, 6–10," in *Calendar of State Papers Colonial*, 302–29.

360. "Charles Scarburgh to Governor Nicholson, May 3, 1700," in *Privateering and Piracy*, 265.

361. Minutes of Council of Virginia, May 6, 1700, "America and West Indies: May 1700, 6–10," in *Calendar of State Papers Colonial*, 229–47.

362. Ibid.; see also Rogers Dey Whichard, *The History of Lower Tidewater, Virginia* (New York: Lewis Historical Publishing Co., 1959), 132.

363. Minutes of Council of Virginia, May 6, 1700, "America and West Indies: May 1700, 6–10," in *Calendar of State Papers Colonial*, 229–47.

364. Ibid.

365. Whichard, *History of Lower Tidewater*, 132.

366. Ibid.

367. Gill, "Short and Violent Career," 39–40.

368. Whichard, History of Lower Tidewater, 132.

369. *See The Trials of John Hougling, Cornelius Franc and Francois Delaunee for Piracies and Robberies by them Committed in a Ship Called the* Peace *in Company and with the Assistance of Several Others, Near the Capes of Virginia*, CO 5/1411.

370. Ibid.

371. Ibid.

372. Ibid.

373. None of the witnesses knew "the persons Indicted by their names," so the grand jury (ibid.):

> *Sent the officer that attended us to move the court that those persons might be sent up to us to see whether the witnesses know them by sight, and he returning without them, the jury have directed me to acquaint this court that 'til we are satisfyed in this matter, we cannot against upon the bills and, therefore, we pray that this court will be pleased to have the indicted persons brought before the court and the witnesses examined whether they know them to be the persons mencioned in the indictment.*
>
> *The court then ordered John Hoogling, Cornelius Frank and Francois Delaunee to be brought to the barr, which was done accordingly, and the witnesses asked severall questions concerning the knowledge of their persons for [t]he satisfaction of the jury who, thereupon, withdrew to consider further the matter before them.*

374. Ibid.

375. Ibid.

376. Ibid.

377. Ibid.; *See also* Gill, "Short and Violent Career," 41.

378. *The Trials of John Hougling, Cornelius Franc and Francois Delaunee for Piracies and Robberies by them Committed in a Ship Called the* Peace *in Company and with the Assistance of Several Others, Near the Capes of Virginia*, CO 5/1411.

379. Gill, "Short and Violent Career," 41.

380. *The Trials of John Hougling, Cornelius Franc and Francois Delaunee for Piracies and Robberies by them Committed in a Ship Called the* Peace *in Company and with the Assistance of Several Others, Near the Capes of Virginia*, CO 5/1411.

381. Rankin, *Golden Age of Piracy*, 74.

382. *The Trials of John Hougling, Cornelius Franc and Francois Delaunee for Piracies and Robberies by them Committed in a Ship Called the* Peace *in Company and with the Assistance of Several Others, Near the Capes of Virginia*, CO 5/1411; see also Gill, "Short and Violent Career," 41.

Chapter 15

383. Testimony of John Staples, *The Trials of John Hougling, Cornelius Franc and Francois Delaunee for Piracies and Robberies by them Committed in a Ship Called the* Peace *in Company and with the Assistance of Several Others, Near the Capes of Virginia*, CO 5/1411.

384. Ibid.

385. Testimony of Jacob Moreland and Testimony of John Staples, *The Trials of John Hougling, Cornelius Franc and Francois Delaunee for Piracies and Robberies by them Committed in a Ship Called the* Peace *in Company and with the Assistance of Several Others, Near the Capes of Virginia*, CO 5/1411.

386. *The Trials of John Hougling, Cornelius Franc and Francois Delaunee for Piracies and Robberies by them Committed in a Ship Called the* Peace *in Company and with the Assistance of Several Others, Near the Capes of Virginia*, CO 5/1411.

387. Ibid.

388. Ibid.

389. Ibid.; see also Whichard, *History of Lower Tidewater*, 132.

Chapter 16

390. Rankin, *Golden Age of Piracy*, 75.

391. Ibid.; "America and West Indies: June 1700, 6–10," in *Calendar of State Papers Colonial*, 302–29.

392. Ibid.

393. Rankin, *Golden Age of Piracy*, 75.
394. Ibid.
395. A Warrant to the Sheriff of Princess Anne County Directing the Place of Execution in these Words, *The Trials of John Hougling, Cornelius Franc and Francois Delaunee for Piracies and Robberies by them Committed in a Ship Called the* Peace *in Company and with the Assistance of Several Others, Near the Capes of Virginia*, CO 5/1411.
396. "John and Adam Thorowgood to Captain Passenger, May 3, 1700," in *Privateering and Piracy*, 266–67.
397. Rankin, *Golden Age of Piracy*, 75–76; "John and Adam Thorowgood to Captain Passenger, May 3, 1700," in *Privateering and Piracy*, 266–67.
398. "John and Adam Thorowgood to Captain Passenger, May 3, 1700," in *Privateering and Piracy*, 266–67.
399. John and Adam Thorowgood were substantial planters of Princess Anne County, dwelling near Lynnhaven Bay and descendants of Adam Thorowgood, who is credited with renaming the Lynnhaven Bay from its original name, Morton's Bay, given to it by John Smith (*linn* or *lynn* refers to a pool, cascade or waterfall, and *haven* refers to an inlet of the sea, the mouth of a river, a harbor or port). The Thorowgood namesake has been carried forward into modern times, although it has been modified to "Thoroughgood," referring to a neighborhood, elementary school and shopping center(s). Other descendants of Adam Thorowgood, including, potentially, Thorowgood's mother or John or Adam Jr., were rumored to own the "Pleasure House" tavern, for which Pleasure House Road in modern-day Virginia Beach is named; "John and Adam Thorowgood to Captain Passenger, May 3, 1700," in *Privateering and Piracy*, 266–67.
400. "John and Adam Thorowgood to Captain Passenger, May 3, 1700," in *Privateering and Piracy*, 266–67.
401. Ibid.
402. Ibid.
403. Ibid.
404. "Benjamin Harrison Jr., to Governor Nicholson, May 4, 1700," in *Privateering and Piracy*, 268.
405. Benjamin Harrison Jr., also known as "Benjamin Harrison of Berkeley," was attorney general of the Virginia colony and son of a member of the Virginia Council, Benjamin Harrison of Surry. Harrison Jr. was also the great-grandfather of President William Henry Harrison (ibid.).
406. Ibid.

407. "William Wilson to Governor Nicholson, May 5, 1700," in *Privateering and Piracy*, 269–70.

408. "Governor Nicholson to Captain Passenger, May 4, 1700," in *Privateering and Piracy*, 268–69.

409. Rankin, *Golden Age of Piracy*, 75–76.

410. Minutes of Council of Virginia, May 7, 1700, "America and West Indies: May 1700, 6–10," *Calendar of State Papers Colonial*, 229–47.

411. Ibid.

412. Ibid.

413. Governor Nicholson to the Council of Trade and Plantations, June 10, 1700, "America and West Indies: June 1700, 6-10," in *Calendar of State Papers Colonial*, 302–29.

414. Minutes of Council of Virginia, May 7, 1700, "America and West Indies: May 1700, 6–10," in *Calendar of State Papers Colonial*, 229–47.

415. Ibid.

416. Ibid.

417. A *libel*, in admiralty law, is a plaintiff's or claimant's document containing his allegations and instituting a suit, similar to a complaint in modern law. "Libel by Captain William Passenger, May 11, 1700," *Privateering and Piracy*, 271–72.

418. Ibid., 271.

419. Sworn and subscribed.

420. "Libel by Captain William Passenger, May 11, 1700," in *Privateering and Piracy*, 271–72.

421. Minutes of Council of Virginia, May 7, 1700, "America and West Indies: May 1700, 6–10," in *Calendar of State Papers Colonial*, 229–47.

422. Gill, "Short and Violent Career," 39.

423. Minutes of Council of Virginia, May 7, 1700, "America and West Indies: May 1700, 6–10," in *Calendar of State Papers Colonial*, 229–47.

424. Ibid.

425. Ibid.

426. Rankin, *Golden Age of Piracy*, 74; Minutes of Council of Virginia, May 6, 1700, "America and West Indies: May 1700, 6–10," in *Calendar of State Papers Colonial*, 229–47. ("Whereas of late there have been several ships taken, plundered or destroyed by pirates hovering over the coasts of this dominion, and information having been given that there is still one or more on the coast, ordered that HMS *Essex Prize* sail on the 30th inst., and give convoy to all merchant ships.")

427. Minutes of Council of Virginia, May 6, 1700, "America and West Indies: May 1700, 6–10," in *Calendar of State Papers Colonial*, 229–47; Governor Nicholson to the Council of Trade and Plantations, June 10, 1700, "America and West Indies: June 1700, 6–10," in *Calendar of State Papers Colonial*, 302–29.

428. Hanna, *Pirate Nests*, 285.

429. Governor Nicholson to the Council of Trade and Plantations, June 10, 1700, "America and West Indies: June 1700, 6–10," in *Calendar of State Papers Colonial*, 302–29.

430. Rankin, *Golden Age of Piracy*, 75.

431. Ibid., 74.

432. Ibid., 75–76.

433. *London Post with Intelligence Foreign and Domestick*, June 10–12, 1700; Rankin, *Golden Age of Piracy*, 75–76.

434. Rankin, *Golden Age of Piracy*, 75–76.

435. Minutes of Council of Virginia, June 5, 1700, "America and West Indies: June 1700, 1–5," in *Calendar of State Papers Colonial*, 296–302.

436. Letter from Governor Blake to the Earl of Jersey, June 10, 1700, "America and West Indies: January 1700, 2–5," in *Calendar of State Papers Colonial*, 1–21.

437. Letter from Mr. Randolph to Mr. Popple, Secretary at the Plantation Office, May 16, 1700, "America and West Indies: May 1700, 16–20," in *Calendar of State Papers Colonial*, 255–62.

438. Letter from Colonel Quary to the Council of Trade and Plantations, June 5, 1700, "America and West Indies: June 1700, 1–5," *Calendar of State Papers Colonial*, 296–302.

439. Ibid.

Epilogue

440. Gill, "Short and Violent Career," 41.

441. Minutes of Council of Virginia, May 7, 1700, "America and West Indies: May 1700, 6–10," *Calendar of State Papers Colonial*, 229–47.

442. Letter from Governor Nicholson to the Council of Trade and Plantations, August 27, 1700, "America and West Indies: August 1700, 26–29," *Calendar of State Papers Colonial*, 494–505.

INDEX

Princess Anne County, Virginia 30, 36, 44, 73, 90, 94, 134
Providence Galley 39, 40, 41, 42, 43

Q

Quakers 24, 37, 90, 94
Quary, Robert 24, 28, 101, 136
Quedagh Merchant 39

R

Rankin, Hugh 29
Rhode Island 21, 22, 25, 34, 46
Rose 21
Rowe, Captain Simon 27, 31, 32, 36

S

Shomette, Donald 68
Shoreham 67, 68, 69, 70, 72, 73, 75, 76, 77, 79, 80, 83, 87, 88, 92, 93, 94, 95, 96, 97, 99, 101, 103, 104, 124, 127, 129
South Carolina 27, 37, 90, 94, 98, 100, 106, 107, 111
Spotswood, Alexander 21, 106
Suffolk, Virginia 30, 90

T

Tangier 20
Tangier Regiment 20
Teach, Edward. *See* Blackbeard
tobacco 23, 37, 69, 71

Tortuga 47, 48, 60, 118
Trade and Plantations, Council of 24, 25, 28, 96
Trade, Board of 27, 107

V

Virginia Beach, Virginia 9, 30, 36, 90, 134

W

Wafer, Lionel 31, 32, 34
West Jersey 25, 29
William and Mary, College of 32
Williamsburg, Virginia 32, 84
Williams, Lloyd Haynes 30

Y

York River 34

ABOUT THE AUTHOR

Monarch Studios.

Jeremy R. Moss is an accomplished real estate developer, lawyer and lobbyist living in Jacksonville, Florida. An emerging author and freelance historian, Jeremy's research is focused on piracy and early colonial maritime history. Jeremy's first book, *The Life and Tryals of the Gentleman Pirate, Major Stede Bonnet*, was met with significant interest and praise. When not working or writing, Jeremy is a family man and can be found telling stories of adventure and buried treasure to his three young sons (www.AuthorJeremyMoss.com).